Panther!

OTHER TITLES BY ROGER A. CARAS
AVAILABLE IN BISON BOOK EDITIONS

The Custer Wolf: Biography of an American Renegade

Monarch of Deadman Bay:
The Life and Death of a Kodiak Bear

Panther!

by ROGER A. CARAS
Illustrations by Charles Fracé

University of Nebraska Press
Lincoln

First Bison Book printing: 1990
Most recent printing indicated by the last digit below:
10   9   8   7   6   5   4   3   2   1

Library of Congress Cataloging-in-Publication Data
Caras, Roger A.
Panther! / by Roger A. Caras: illustrations by Charles Fracé. — 1st
Bison Book print.
p.   cm.
Reprint. Originally published: 1st ed. Boston: Little, Brown and
Co., c1969.
ISBN 0-8032-6338-4
I. Title.
PS3553.A64P36   1990
813'.54—dc20
90-36841   CIP

Reprinted by arrangement with Roger A. Caras

For Clay, who will understand . . .

Panther!

🌿 1 🌿

IT WAS AN HOUR BEFORE SUNSET AND THE OPEN WATER leads between the tufts of saw grass reflected the pre-storm sky. The yellow sea spread out in every direction, more than a million acres of it. Along the horizon the earth's dark breasts rose in the form of hammocks, slight features in the midst of the sedge flats, whose increased elevation of even a few feet enabled a totally different kind of vegetation to grow there. The constituent trees of the forests crowding the hammock brows could not be distinguished, for their combined mass appeared now in silhouette.

The larger birds had come to roost. The barometric pressure was dropping and the wind had already started soughing in the mangrove jungles that marked the seaward boundaries to the west of the Everglades. The mistlike egrets knew, the herons — Louisiana, blue, green, and black-crowned night — the spoonbills, and the ibises, they knew, too, and had come to perch before the storm crossed the edge of the land and imperiled their flight. Low across the sea of saw grass the water turkey, Anhinga, pushed, anxious to find a suitable pond with thick weeds at its borders. His unimpressive grunts trailed behind him, punctuated by a stream of excrement. Four pelicans in formation flew overhead at a thousand feet, exhibiting the only grace they knew, the grace of flight. Off beyond where the grass opened and a slough worked its way south toward the sea, a limpkin called in his strange mimicry of madness. But then he fell silent, almost as if he were ashamed of what he had said, and an alligator took him from behind. The splash was barely audible and only a cruising gar knew of the event.

Six muscular feet of eastern diamondback rattlesnake broke off in the middle of an S-shaped thrust and twisted back into a coil. A nervous tail rose straight up, ready to sound the warning. The lanceolate head held rigidly six inches off the ground and malevolent, unblinking eyes focused in the direction of the disturbance. The snake's inquiring tongue joined the search and before long enough of the telltale particles of odor had accumulated with the other evidence. The snake adjusted his coils, drew his head back a little farther to tighten the spring and his tail began to vibrate. The panther would pass close to him, too close, and the snake was ready to defend himself against the spontaneous flick of a paw that could end his life. He had the speed — and the venom — to balance the other's wit.

The panther, though, had other things to concern him and at the first warning buzz angled away from the infuriated snake. Several times in the course of his wanderings that day, he had scented a female, and although he had lost the trail back in a tangle of marshy streams and surface water, experience directed him toward the hammock, the nearest one that rose higher out of the grass as he approached it.

A thousand yards short of the hammock, on a small dry mound, he stopped to sort things out and sat back on his haunches, waiting for a signal, a sound of some kind, perhaps, or the sight of a tawny coat. In a kind of displacement activity he bent forward and rasped his tongue through the fur on his shoulder and then raised his forepaw and concentrated on it. He stopped his work and listened, his tongue still extended, his leg raised and his head twisted down to meet it. But there were no signals yet and he continued his grooming for several more minutes before moving forward again. As he walked, the muscles of his shoulders rippled outward to form wave patterns on his skin. His long, downward-arching tail twitched occasionally at the end, the only sign he gave that there was anything at all on his mind.

Even after he had her scent, the male panther's approach to his prospective mate was oblique and cautious. The cat's personality does not lend itself to direct approaches. There is a kind of ritual in the initial contact that makes disinterest and casualness, or at least the appearance of these two qualities, imperative. An exception would occur only if the male contemplated attacking the stranger, and that was the farthest thing from his mind.

And so began the cat-and-cat game, the intense magnification of the cat-and-mouse play that is so essentially a part of the cat's complicated personality. For two hours, until well after the sun had slipped down into the Gulf of Mexico beyond the bordering mangrove tangles, the two cats played their game of disinterest and disdain. They were never out of reach of each other's signals, never really very far apart, but she wouldn't acknowledge him and he would hardly have let it be known that his very being was swelling and aching for the want of her. What actually was the inbred caution of the predatory animal, an outcast in every society, appeared to be supreme ego, but that was only a facade, as is so much of what man believes to be his understanding of the cat family, animals that cannot really be understood at all.

The storm that had worried the larger birds well in advance of its approach began pushing gulf water shoreward beneath the arching mangrove roots. Low ridges of white water licked at the shore and sudden swirlings showed where fish were turning away from the shallows and heading for deeper troughs where they would be safe. Within a half hour after sunset the first tentative sightings had given way to authentic gusts and the winds that had begun in northern highlands and had crossed broad lands reached the boundary of the Glades again and temperature followed pressure in a downward spiral. As the male panther finally turned inward toward the hammock to where the female waited, the first rain fell. In minutes it changed from a vertical shower to a slashing horizontal deluge. As the storm drilled into the woods, the panther emerged from between two trees and stared balefully with lustrous eyes. The female looked at him for an instant and then paced off into a deeper place, knowing that he would follow.

The next time the male panther emerged into a small clearing the female held her ground. They were in the hammock now and somewhat protected from the rain. Water dripped from every leaf and slithered down the trunks of the trees, but the slashing of the wind was ameliorated by the thickness of the growth. As the male approached, the female's tail twitched a constant rhythm. She was on her side, panting, breathing heavily through her open mouth while a rasping lament issued from deep within her. When he was ten feet off she rolled her lips back, wrinkled her muzzle and spit halfheartedly. Her ears lay back along her head. As befitted his position in life, he ignored her and lay down six feet off, then began peeping like a small bird. Exactly that, comic as it would have appeared to a human intruder, the great male cat stared at his prospective mate with yellow satin eyes and chirped and peeped like a slightly oversized canary. In an act of apparent disdain she flung herself over onto her back, squirmed once or twice and rolled the other way, presenting him with her shoulder. In an imitative action he did much the same thing, rolling over, working his shoulders into the ground, but when he came to rest he was three feet closer to his goal. He lay watching her, staring fixedly at the back of her neck before standing and moving toward her. He stood over her for a minute and then reached down and bit her firmly in the scruff. She spun with an explosive hiss and struck out with her great right forepaw. He dodged the blow and she sank back and stared at him. He raised his right foreleg and tentatively slapped her across the side of the head. It was less a blow than a caress. She rolled over flat on the ground and waited for his next suggestive advance. She was the very essence of sensuality, her every move a plea for domination.

Overhead and beyond the protective margins of the hammock the wind shifted to the northwest and the rain clouds moved off toward the Atlantic. As quickly as it had appeared, the storm passed. Its violence had been brief; the rainfall had appeared to be more drenching than it was because of the wind. The sky was clear across the enormous table-flat expanse of the Everglades. The night animals moved out from cover and began the business of the dark hours. The hunters stalked their prey and the prey practiced their evasive tactics, but there were those that had to die. Some did so quietly, wheezing out of life with soft flutterings and shudders while others were noisier about it, less willing to accept their fate with resignation. Their tremulous squealings were heard in a thousand places, but not an ounce of sympathy was engendered in the land.

While the other creatures of the Everglades feasted upon each other, the two panthers continued their foreplay. However it may have appeared, their play was not a game but an essential prelude to the business of creating a future generation in kind. The female alternately invited and rejected her suitor with purrs and soft hummings one minute and violent outbursts of spitting the next. He was as fickle as she. One moment he would be caressing, cajoling, and the next he would slap her or nip her painfully on the flank or scruff. All of this, of course, had a purpose. It heightened the intensity of their desire and assured the successful completion of the sexual act. The female was receptive, in heat after a twenty-three-day interestrus.

There was a time when the male would have had to fight very nearly to the death for the possession of this female, but the panther population is thin enough in Florida now to make such violent battles between competing males less likely to occur. For the eight or nine days of her heat the female was a highly desirable object and any male that happened across her track was sure to seek her out. This single male, though, was the only one within a radius of a dozen miles and he had her to himself without contention.

The desire of the two animals to join was increasing in intensity, yet the ritual that marked their meeting had to be played out according to the rules. The cubs that would result from this meeting would not be delayed by the few hours of play that preceded the mating, but they might be better examples of their species, assured of a full heritage by the display of which both parents proved themselves capable.

The lure-taunt-pursuit-reject pattern carried the two panthers across the hammock and back. They were totally absorbed in the business at hand and took little note of the other inhabitants of the pocket forest, although these observers were profoundly disturbed by both the incessant movement of the two cats and the increasing volume of sound that accompanied their play. A bobcat, a tough creature in his own right, chose the wisest course available to him and left the hammock altogether. In so doing he exhibited the kind of discretion that had enabled him to live successfully in the shadow of a larger cat for nearly twenty years. Birds huddling in every tree moved nervously along their branches and many sought higher levels. Only a barn owl refused to be intimidated and turned his head from side to side with enormous eyes approximating an expression of scandalized indignation. After the panthers had moved away from under his tree and he had proved his point, he swung off his branch and sailed out across the saw grass like a giant moth. He dropped and took a water rat after a thousand yards. In his way he was a panther, too, a panther of the skies.

The game continued to increase in intensity and yowling replaced spitting and hissing as the biting and slapping became rougher. At the point in their play where any increase in violence would have caused significant damage, the two cats mated. The act itself was hardly less boisterous than what had gone before, but it was accomplished at last and as the first rays of morning light reached the hammock from the east, the male panther stood at its edge and stared out across the open flat. He began wandering aimlessly away from the high ground but quickly adjusted his course until with purpose in his stride he headed for another hammock he knew well, two miles away. Back where he had left her the female bedded down and after tending to several particularly painful bites and scratches, she slept.

Twice more in the next five days the two cats met, both times out in the open. They mated the first time, after an abbreviated foreplay of only two hours, but the second and last time they only rubbed against each other, purring loudly. It was over and they both had other things to occupy their time and their energies. The male would wander in his endless search for prey and perhaps find another mate receptive to him. The female had ninety-six days to prepare for the coming of her cubs. If she met another male in the first day or two, she might mate with him as well, depending on her mood. But that wasn't to be. By the time she next encountered a male panther her heat had passed and the chemistry that prompted it lay dormant until immediately after the birth of her cubs. Her conscious knowledge of what had occurred and its consequence were virtually nonexistent, yet through her instincts she was capable of preparing for it with as much skill as if the whole scheme had been of her own design. She didn't have to understand; her species did. The system had been put to the test a million times and more and had never been found wanting.

≫ 2 ≪

THE LAND WHERE THE FEMALE PANTHER ROAMED IS A strange one, a unique subtropical wilderness of nearly twenty-two hundred square miles. Time and again, more times than we shall probably ever know, the land there has been reclaimed by the sea. Each time the water rolled back again, another layer of sediment was left behind to cover the rocks of the peninsula. Slowly, the porous land evolved as an enormous basin sloping toward the south and west. For centuries, rain and drainage from Lake Okeechobee to the north were kept from seeping down through the underlying limestone by a cover of marl and peat. The great spillage from Okeechobee's depressed southern boundary did not form into rivers as it ran to the sea, but flowed across the land. The limestone outcroppings that appear to the north and east are now the foundations of southern Florida's cities, and where they appear in the Everglades itself they are the hammocks upon which the hardwoods, ferns and air plants grow.

The elevation within the Glades varies from sea level to ten feet. Even these very slight variations are enough to create the several distinctly different habitats into which the region is divided: willow swamps, hammocks, sloughs, cypress jungles, saw-grass flats and pine flatwoods. The entire ecosystem is tied to water supply, for the Everglades is first and foremost a land of water. Without a steady supply the animals there sicken and die and the sky is blackened by the smoke of grass fires. Here the land must be wet or it dies.

The Everglades is a transitional zone, linking the continental floristic provinces of North America with that of the West Indies. The exchange of vectors, water, wind and birds with the islands to the south has resulted in a mixed system unique on our continent. The saw grass, often ten feet high, is closely related to sedges found in New Jersey bogs, while the mastic and gumbo-limbo trees are essentially West Indian species. Botanically, the Everglades is a melting pot.

Plant life competes with itself no less than do animal forms in the Everglades. Competition has driven many of the orchids and other air plants up into the trees and forced the wild mangroves out to the edge of the sea, where they alone can survive ankle-deep in the warm brine of the Gulf. The

coastal features of the area are products of the mangrove's retreat in no small part. The seeds of the red mangrove, the
island builders, germinate while still aloft and often hang on
until the embryonic root is a foot or more long. If the ground
is exposed when the seedling falls, it plants itself. If the tide
is in or the water high, it floats root down until it reaches exposed land, where it establishes itself in the ooze. It grows
rapidly, with arching roots forming a thick tangle. Floating
debris and animal colonies are caught and established until the
beginnings of a new island are formed. In effect the trees have
retreated from the fierce competition of the land and gone to
sea, where they can form their own world.

It is a rich land and life is produced in incredible profusion
and variety. Fifty species of mosquitoes inhabit the area. They
have evolved so that the competition between them is limited.
They have specialized their habits so that they are active at
different times of the day and night. A third of all the ferns
found in the United States are found in Florida; sixty of these
hundred are of tropical origin and are limited to the region of
the Everglades. The area is their single toehold in the United
States. Three hundred and twenty-three species of birds have
been recorded in the region, two hundred and twenty-seven
occur regularly, eighty nest there. The native butterflies and
skippers number one hundred and forty-two, and the amphib-
ians sixteen. The reptiles number fifty, including such dramatic forms as the alligator, the few remaining North American crocodiles, and the eastern diamondback rattlesnake,
potentially one of the dozen or so most dangerous snakes in
the world.

Ten species of whale and dolphin have been found in waters

rimming the peninsula and thirty-seven mammals inhabit the land, the most dramatic of these undeniably being the cat they call panther. Elsewhere the same cat is called mountain lion, puma, cougar, screamer and catamount, but in Florida the name is panther, or sometimes "painter" in its corrupted form. The female specimen that mated that troubled night, one of perhaps two hundred-odd surviving panthers in the region, weighed one hundred and five pounds. From the tip of her nose to the darkened end of her three-foot tail she measured a total of exactly eight feet. She stood an even three feet at the withers, two inches higher in the rump. As is generally the case with Florida panthers, she was darker, richer, a more distinctly reddish-brown than cats of her species found to the north and west. The mountain lions of Arizona, Colorado, California and Montana are pale in comparison to the short, stiff rufous hairs that constituted most of her coat. Her ears, like the tip of her tail, were dark and shone from deep cinnamon to black, depending on the light. Her belly was white, as was her rump, to the first hind-leg joint. Her upper lips near the sides of her nose, her chin and throat, were nearly pure white, with pinkish-buff overtones on the underside of her neck. The sides of her neck were a cinnamon-pink buff, as were her feet. The light played tricks with her colors and what might appear at first glimpse to be a fairly uniformly colored cat was in fact an intricate blending of subtle, muted tones.

In most ways, though, she resembled all of the other mountain lions of North and South America. She had large paws armed with devastatingly sharp claws, five on each front foot, four on each rear. They were an inch long and gave her enormous gripping power. She was graceful, sleek and strangely mysterious, a perfect specimen of her kind in appearance and behavior. She was an outstanding example of an outstandingly successful species. Her kind has the greatest north-south range of any species of cat in the world. They are found today, as they have been for untold thousands of years, from almost the very southern tip of South America up into Canada. They are found in deserts, swamps, mountain valleys and deep forests. Like all of her species, the panther who bred that night less than forty miles west of Miami Beach was sly, secretive, adaptable, inventive and sure. She was a consummate stalker and still hunter, a climber capable of leaping fifteen feet or more straight up onto the trunk of a tree, and a sprinter. On flat land she could bound forward in twenty-foot leaps; from a standstill she could broadjump nearly fifteen feet. When necessary she could swim with speed and determination. It was a combination of her appearance and these qualities that made of her a coveted big-game trophy throughout her species's range. These same qualities had the power to engender fear and resentment. It was well known that she could, despite her small size, kill a fifty-pound colt with one pounce and carry it for three miles before tiring. A thousand-pound horse was hardly a challenge for her and she could, if necessary, drag it over a fence or into a ravine. Although her speed could be accounted for by her form, her strength seemed hardly possible for so small a cat. She was, after all, only a quarter the size of a tigress. Her secret lay in her internal structure. She was a completely economical combination of bone, sinew and muscle. Nothing was wasted, nothing was extra and no important elements were missing. In thousands of generations nature had devised a perfect killing machine, a swift, sure, fiercely determined feline predator whose intent on staying alive was matched by her ability to do so.

The Everglades was just one of the hundreds of specialized habitats in which the panther could have been at home. But thousands of years earlier her ancestors had discovered this place, found it rewardingly stocked with a variety of animal foods, and here they had prospered. Her kind was now a balancing element in the ecology of the area: she had a job to do, for her killing was a part of the natural scheme. Except in rare instances the animals on which she preyed had a birth rate to accommodate her depredations. The Everglades was lacking nothing of what she needed. Sleek, sure, generally silent and excessively shy, she was the great trimmer, the unrelenting reaper, the great cat of the Florida southern swamp.

🌿 3 🌿

THE WATER ON THREE SIDES OF BILLY BUCK ISLAND WAS SIX inches deep. Only on the west side, where a slough ran to the south, was wading uncomfortable for the female panther. The island, actually a hammock just under a half mile in length and seventy yards wide on the average, was at the center of her hunting range. The elongated limestone oval ran north and south and its edges were indented by narrow channels leading to gator pools in its interior. The channels and the pools, solution holes nowhere more than five or six feet deep, were well hidden from the outside world. Each was a private world unto itself, and a primeval one. Each was a silent place that time had yet to discover.

Ever since parting from her mate the female had remained close to her hammock. Three weeks had passed and she was beginning to sense the changes taking place within her body, but her behavior remained the same as before, with one exception. Slowly the instinct to establish a den, to seek a permanent place, was awakening. Under normal circumstances she would range as much as fifteen miles in a single day, but since breeding she had seldom moved as much as five.

An island in a sea that is six inches deep is quite different from other islands. The panther was not isolated. Prey animals attuned to the peculiar Everglades characteristic of surface water waded freely from hammock to hammock and each day brought new hunting opportunities. A bobcat moving onto a hammock a mile away would drive the deer off after a day or two and Billy Buck was as likely to be the recipient of the emigrants as any other hammock in the area.

At the southern end of the island a hidden pool nearly fifty feet across was the site of an Anhinga nesting colony and raccoons came there regularly in search of the water turkeys' eggs. The fact that many of the smaller hunters never left the island could teach others of their kind nothing. In a land where there is an exchange of hunters as well as an exchange of prey animals from island to island, there are no lessons to be learned from a vanished individual. The population is too fluid.

The raccoon is a hunting animal, constantly seeking small water creatures, birds, smaller mammals and reptiles. Although alert and cautious, he will on occasion make the fatal mistake of becoming so involved in the hunt that he forgets that he himself may one day be prey to another and larger animal. Swifter than a raccoon, a far better climber, as good a swimmer and several times his weight, the panther found little difficulty in taking a few raccoons every week. At least once a week a deer breaking through the hammock's perimeter from the sea of grass beyond fell to her skill. The cubs growing within her created new demands upon her system and she hunted constantly, killing at least once a day. Even without a visiting deer or coon the hammock provided more than enough for her and her growing needs.

Eighty yards north of the Anhinga pool there was another one only slightly smaller. At the edge of this an alligator had built her nest over a year before. She had remained near the large mound of twigs and leaf debris for three months, until the characteristic high-pitched grunting sound from within had told her that the several dozen large white eggs she had deposited in the spring had begun to hatch. With a sudden burst of energy the eleven-foot giant had torn the nest apart, allowing the six- and seven-inch hatchlings to escape the humid warmth of the decaying vegetation. Once the babies were free and began finding their way down to the pool, the mother abandoned them. Three nights later, while hunting gar in the slough to the west, she was jacked, shot and skinned by poachers who would realize five dollars a running foot for her belly skin.

The young alligators had each grown between twelve and eighteen inches in their first year and twenty of them still remained on the island or in its immediately surrounding waters when the female panther moved in. At least once a week she

killed one of the young saurians, although mammalian prey
would have sustained her easily enough. Perhaps she sought
variety in her diet, for the tough little reptiles offered little
actual return on her efforts.

Marsh rabbits, otters, skunks and the peculiar little Everglades mink were regular inhabitants or frequent visitors and
provided additional food. She was also adept at taking the
larger wading birds, although as her gestation period advanced
she became less and less prone to exert herself for such small
rewards. There was little need. Billy Buck Island was a feast
reset each day.

The highest point on the hammock was a broad ridge down
its center, less than four feet above average water level. Even
in floodtime the crest of the ridge remained dry and secure.
Near the north end a dozen red-barked gumbo-limbo trees
clustered together and formed a tight forest in miniature. Its
interior was dark and safe. It was here the panther chose her
den site. It was here her cubs would be born.

In addition to the gumbo-limbo trees (immigrants from the
West Indies), the strangler fig, pigeon plum, sweet bay, coco
plum, sweet acacia and wild tamarind grew to add to the im-
penetrability of the ridge growth. Further along the ridge wild
fruit trees grew, dropping their fruit to the ground year after
year, attracting the smaller rodents who in turn brought reptiles in pursuit. It was a thick, wild place, one well suited to the
panther's needs.

At the extreme northern end of the hammock there was a
bowl-like depression a hundred feet in diameter. On the ridge
surrounding it there had once been a small Seminole settlement of a dozen people and in the bowl itself the remains of

their cornfield and their indian-pumpkin patch continued to grow in disorderly profusion. To this site wild pigs came, some of them of immense size. These feral giants were descendants of domesticated strains that had been established on farmlands to the east and north a hundred years earlier. Their ancestors, escaping, had spread toward the southwest, where they were less likely to be hunted and where the watery world of the Everglades kept dogs from coming on their own account. The tough, aggressive descendants of European breeds snuffled from hammock to hammock, taking what they could find. They did not die as easily as a deer, raccoon or rabbit, but the rewards they offered the predator strong enough and brave enough to face their slashing tusks were great and the female panther came here to hunt as well.

On a bright sunlit morning in the fifth week of her gestation the panther moved along the island's central ridge toward the Indian settlement. The wading birds who roosted on the island were off stalking the shallows in search of prey of their own and only the chittering of smaller songbirds and the low hum of the island's insect population broke the silence. She slipped through a thick tangle at the edge of the abandoned village and was attracted by the rustling of several rats that were working through a kitchen midden, when a more enticing sound caught her attention. Even before she began her stalk on the rats she swung through one of the thatch-roofed pole huts and leaped easily onto a wooden platform that had once served as a bed for an entire Seminole family. On another platform nearby a white-footed mouse scurried to safety, and off on a piece of planking a ground rattler disturbed in his early-morning sunning ritual drew up tighter, ready to defend himself. But the panther was not interested in either mice or rattlesnakes. She could hear several pigs snuffling and grunting below, where the stunted indian corn still grew.

She sank down on the bed platform and listened for several minutes. The pigs were rooting and feeding and would be easy to stalk, if not easy to kill. As silent as the rays of sunlight that filtered through the wind-tears in the thatch overhead, she slipped off the platform, avoided the hysterically angry ground rattler and moved around the perimeter of the bowl. She kept herself well hidden from below and instinctively chose the downwind side of the arena. The pigs could scent her at least as well as she could scent them, but she had one great advantage over them. She was a ghost, a silent shadow on cat feet in the deep growth, and they were noisy, carelessly broadcasting their every move. On the far side of the depression, opposite the center of the old village, she slipped in closer, using a fallen tree as a shield. Hunching down, she was able to look out through a tangle of low-growing shrubs and watch her prey's movements. Up to that point she had been following them by ear alone. Now she could see them as well and better judge her stalk.

In some indefinable way the pigs began to sense her presence, or at least to sense that something was wrong. They continued their rooting but looked up more often now and grunted loudly to themselves or perhaps to each other. The basin was the most open land area on the hammock and to move off onto the sedge flats beyond would require that they first penetrate extremely thick growth. This they were unwilling to do as long as their uneasiness was still vague and without direction. The panther took advantage of their growing confusion and inched forward carefully. She knew from experience, and from instinct perhaps, that they would continue to mill around in the basin until they caught sight of her or until the wind shifted and gave her position away. Like string puppets they danced before her as she played her cat game with consummate skill.

Several minutes passed and the pigs' uneasiness began to wane. Without being able to find a specific source of danger they returned to their conscientious feeding, looking up less and less often as their feeble memories of the near-panic of only minutes before began to fade. The panther held her ground.

Suddenly a furious buzzing filled the depression. A half-grown sow had rooted in close to where a six-and-a-half-foot diamondback rattler lay coiled in the sun and he had erupted in fury. Before the sow could react, an enormous pink and black boar shouldered her aside and grabbed the snake by the middle. The snake swung and struck the boar in the face again and again as he calmly proceeded to eat it alive. The sound of the pig's powerful jaws crushing the snake and his own grunting and slobbering were carried clearly to the panther's hiding place and she squirmed her hindquarters in anticipation of the charge.

His face was already beginning to swell as the boar grunted and stamped his way across the low depression, gulping the still-living snake down a foot at a time. His head was high as he moved toward the panther and his left eye, only inches from one of the five places where the dying rattler had struck, was already swollen shut. Too late the pig saw the bushes move. With two feet of rattlesnake still dangling from his jaws he swung to meet the charge, but the panther feinted to the side and took the six-hundred-pound boar in the shoulder, well clear of its slashing tusks. With a heavy, windy grunt the pig went down on his side. The panther's right paw, working faster than could be clearly seen, shot forward and hooked the pig in the snout. Releasing her hold on his shoulder, she snapped shut on his throat just as his neck snapped. Her furiously pumping hind legs already had his belly open in several foot-long parallel slits. She stepped across him and watched with emotionless yellow eyes as he kicked convulsively several times, tried to stand and rolled over on his side with a final heaving sigh. It had been a superbly executed assassination.

At the first appearance of the panther the other pigs scattered in wild confusion and plowed headlong through the old village. As poles were brushed aside by crashing bodies, thatched roofs caved inward. The dust rose in a cloud of swirling motes, climbing rays of sunlight that filtered down through the trees overhead. The lizard and rodent population of the thatch flew in all directions as panic gripped their miniworld. The crashing of the madly plunging pigs was soon lost in the dense thicket and the cat turned again to her prey. Her tail was lashing back and forth and she held her head low. It would be several minutes before her excitement would pass and she would be able to eat in peace. Beyond the edge of the hammock the frantic pigs were bounding through the shallow water toward another, smaller hammock less than a mile away. It would be weeks before any one of the pack would venture back onto Billy Buck, but there would be others for the panther to hunt. There always were.

❧ 4 ❧

IT WAS A TIME LIKE ALL OTHERS IN THE EVERGLADES, A
time of life and death, when the first cub was eased out into
the world. It was a little after midnight and as the female panther turned to examine him, a barn owl swooped low over the
trees on an important errand. The panther knew at once, as
soon as she had opened the sac, that this cub must be discarded.
By some incredible means she knew his back was deformed
and that he could never survive except, perhaps, briefly at her
teat. She struggled to her feet and picked him up in her jaws

and carried him off about ten feet, where she put him down gently on a pile of weedy debris. He rolled on his back and kicked his feet helplessly in the air. She stared down at him for a minute, moaning to herself, then picked him up again and ate him. Then she went back into her sheltered bower to await the birth of further cubs.

Two more cubs were born. A female first, followed half an hour later by a robust male weighing fifteen ounces, two more than his sister. The cubs measured nine inches from their noses to the tips of their stumpy ringed tails. Their woolly coats were spotted and their eyes were closed. It would be at least a week before they would be able to differentiate between light and dark. But they were well born, they had survived, and after resting for a few minutes each began the insistent squealing that would punctuate all the hours of their early days. They were hungry. Their mother had eight mammae, four in her pectoral region, the front two of which were nonfunctioning, two abdominal and two inguinal, so food supply was no problem. Actually she could, with some difficulty perhaps, have fed as many as six cubs, although such litters are extremely rare among her kind.

There was nothing but the warmth of their mother's body, nothing but the milk she supplied, for the first days of the cubs' lives. They ate endlessly, slept all the time they were not nursing, and grew rapidly. By the end of his fourth day the male cub had increased from fifteen to twenty-two ounces. At the end of his eleventh day he weighed an even two pounds. Small slits showed the milky blue eyes beyond that could not yet distinguish shapes but did now know light from dark.

There was a quiet but essential monotony to the cubs' existence in those first weeks. They were laying the physical foundation for their lives and their principal task was to grow. There would be learning ahead, a great deal of that, and there would be play that really was a part of learning. But all that was still weeks away.

The female panther fasted for the first four days of her cubs' new lives. Shortly after dawn on the fifth day she allowed them to nurse until they fell asleep. When their insistent, almost panicky thrusting and pushing against her ceased, she stood up, allowing them to fall off her nipples and roll over on the ground. They didn't waken and she slipped out from under the brush tangle and moved down her regular hunting trail. Because she had not been hunting the area for several days, there were a number of small animals about. They were careless and she took a marsh rabbit easily. He was barely aware of a disturbance nearby before he was dead. She sniffed his enticingly warm carcass, then lay down heavily on her side. She fondled the dead rabbit between her great forepaws and tossed him playfully into the air half a dozen times. Finally she drew him to her and rested her cheek on his limp body as she hugged it. She purred with contentment and nuzzled in against her prize. She bit into it several times and then sniffed happily at the blood that showed. It was her favorite smell at all times, except for those occasions in her life when the hot spicy aroma of an aroused male cat was even more exciting.

She didn't eat the rabbit but played with it for several minutes, filling her nostrils with blood. Then she moved off in search of bigger prey.

By the time she was a thousand yards from her den she began to worry and circled back. She stopped often to listen and although she heard nothing to alarm her, she was uncomfortable away from her cubs. Finally she stopped for the last time, bounded forward in enormous fifteen- and eighteen-foot leaps, stopping only long enough to scoop up her rabbit. When she slipped in under the low-hanging branches, she found her cubs still tumbled as she had left them. She flopped down nearby and ate the rabbit while watching them in their sleep.

By the time six weeks had passed a number of important changes had occurred in the cubs' lives. Sharp little teeth had erupted along the ridges of their gums and they were beginning to gnaw on scraps of meat their mother was bringing to them daily. Their eyes were fully open and in their games, for they now played several hours each day, they used their power of sight to good advantage. The rings on their tails and the spots on their bodies were still distinct. It would be several weeks before their cub markings would even begin to fade and it would be a full year before the last ghosts of their juvenile splotches would vanish. But their body shapes were emerging. They were beginning to look somewhat like cats.

The stubby, undistinguished tails that had characterized them at birth were beginning to show some signs of their future grace and luxuriance. They were growing and there was a hint of the elegant arc they would one day describe. Their paws were immense and their claws, extendable at will, were needle-sharp and perhaps used too often in their play. The areas around their mother's nipples were covered with a mass of tiny scabs where their claws had kneaded their way into her flesh as they nursed. At first she had been tolerant of these small pains, but as the time of their weaning approached she was harshly responsive when they dug their claws into her belly. In fact, she was beginning to exercise her authority and they began to understand her vocabulary. There were times when she was the source of pleasure and times when she meant only pain to them. The cubs, of course, couldn't appreciate the concept of education, but they were learning what was expected of them and the many things that were forbidden.

At nine weeks the young panthers were being led further away from their den each day. They had watched their mother kill rabbits and once a big boar raccoon; they had also seen her react with startlingly bad temper when she found a rattler coiled in her regular pathway not far from their den. She moved faster than they had ever seen her move before and drew back in terror, watching the disabled rattler twist its four feet of lean muscular body into a mass of convulsive coils as if looking for its own head, which now bulged as a mass of torn and disfigured tissue. The harsh rattling noise died and the snake's body relaxed, twisted as it lay upside down with its broad ventral plates glistening in the sun. The panther flicked the carcass off the trail and passed on with her cubs, who soon forgot the episode and began pouncing on their mother's tail, their favorite game of all.

On one occasion the panther left her cubs on a slope at the westward edge of the hammock. Some deer had moved in a little to the south after crossing at night from another, much smaller island a few miles away. She whistled meaningfully to the cubs and moved off. They now had had enough experience to know that the signal she had given meant *stay put.* As their mother moved out of sight the cubs began to play. It was their immediate response to all moments of leisure. When they weren't doing something else, something very specific like sleeping, eating or following their mother in her wanderings after prey, they were playing. The games were basic — tug-of-war with anything that could be found (animal pelts or scraps were, of course, preferred), pounce-and-devastate, eat-ear, chew-and-pursue-flicking-tail, slap-and-hiss, tumble-and-roll, stalk-and-rush — all constituent movements, variations on the theme of hunt-and-kill that would engage them as long as they lived.

Their games this day carried them back and forth over a small clearing at the hammock's edge, no more than twenty-five feet across. The distance from the water's edge to the line of dense vegetation leading into the island's interior was no more than twelve feet. It was a small arena but large enough for a particularly violent game of charge-and-countercharge, so involved, in fact, that they failed to see or hear a slight disturbance at the water's edge.

It was an adult alligator whose ancestors, probably looking very much as he looked that day, arose nearly two hundred million years ago. Never having undergone a spectacular course of evolution, his kind are steady but not dominant elements in the ecology of tropical and some subtropical regions. Within their range they are a timeless constant, always there insofar as man will allow.

The bull that had been cruising twenty yards off the shore was five feet long. He watched the panther move away from the shore and began moving in, totally submerged except for the lumps over his eyes, and his nostrils. From time to time his back and the keels along his powerful sculling tail showed as well, but the cubs were not paying attention to anything but themselves and their game.

About ten yards off, the alligator submerged completely and reappeared again with his chin resting on dry land. Still the cubs were unaware and the alligator waited for their play to bring them closer. Several times it appeared as if their tumbling would roll them down right into the alligator's jaws, but each time some kind of guardian spirit reversed their direction and sent them scrambling to safety, oblivious to the miracle of their escape. Either one would have made little more than an easy mouthful.

If two hundred million years can teach an animal anything, it is patience. The alligator waited. There was no petulant head-bobbing, no exasperated grunts. His metallic eyes followed the cubs' play and judged their movements. Sooner or later one or both would come close enough. He could wait.

Finally, the female managed to get in a particularly good bite on one of the male's ears. He leaped away with a half-hiss, half-yowl, and began circling for a good position from which to get his revenge. He arched his back and looked as intimidating as he knew how. She kept feinting to keep him from gaining the initiative and held her ground at the center of a circle. Round and round the male cub moved, looking for an opening, building his nerve for the charge. The female began edging downhill, knowing from experience that he might suddenly vanish into the brush to emerge a second later and catch her off guard. She wanted him well out in the open, which meant down closer to the water.

The male cub was looking only at his sister, for she was the only danger he recognized for the moment. His downhill swing carried him close to the water, fewer than three feet from its edge, when he was paralyzed by an explosive roar. He could literally feel the alligator's breath as the great beast exhaled with the might of a steam locomotive. In one sudden movement the alligator was up on all four legs, standing on the shore and leaning forward into a rush that would end the cub's life in a second or two at the most. The small cat was less than a third of the alligator's body length away, when the female panther burst out of the brush beside the clearing and with a scream that can only be described as like nothing else at all in this entire world, struck the reptile on the side of the head and turned him halfway around.

The cub recoiled and scrambled up the slope when he saw his mother's body streak forward from the brush. As the cub tumbled to safety, whimpering in terror, the alligator spun to face the panther, lashing the ground behind him bare with his armored tail. His mouth was open and his breath roared out in fury. Only the flames were missing, for here, truly, was a dragon.

The panther was enraged beyond all reason. Her ears lay back along her skull, her tail lashed and her eyes were fiery. She edged sideways in a peculiar crablike battle posture, for the alligator was no deer that could be rushed and downed, no snake that could be flicked into oblivion beside the trail. If she did not kill the alligator, he would kill and most assuredly eat her. Of course, she could have given the retreat signal and bounded off with her cubs into the woods, where the reptile couldn't or at least wouldn't attempt to follow, but her anger, her primeval fury, had taken her far beyond that point. There was to be a death that afternoon. The cat was a recent species, the alligator an ancient one. But both were predators, both killers, both relentless, both fully equipped for combat.

The panther moved down the slope and toward the alligator. He turned to face her. She thus put herself between the giant and the water. Twice he rushed her and twice she flew into the air and came down nearby, still with her back arched, still with her legs stiff, still with her head twisted to the side. Then, suddenly, she charged and pounded the alligator across the snout with a trip-hammer blow. His jaws had been open to grab her paw, but she had been the quicker. The reptile weighed almost four times as much as the cat, but she was infinitely faster-thinking and her timing was better calculated. To a nonpredator his skill would have been incomparable. To her it was primitive. She knew his game much better than he did. As long as they were on open ground she had the advantage. Only in water, where he could submerge and reappear when not expected, would she be totally outclassed.

Again she struck, and again. Each time she managed to hammer a single blow onto his snout. At last she struck higher on his head and tore his right eye out of its socket. His hissing now reached an incredible crescendo, but she was strangely silent. Now she wanted only to kill.

Somehow she understood the peculiarity of the alligator's jaws. If they clamped shut on any part of her, no power she could summon would get him to open them. The power in his jaws on the clamp was incredible. However, once his jaws were closed he had only the weakest of muscles for pulling them apart again. It would be a matter of no contest at all for her to disable him, as long as she avoided the dreadful sweep of his tail.

He charged ineffectively and she bluffed one or two passes herself. The land was torn up now by his thrashing. The birds that had been perching in trees nearby had lathered themselves into a gossiping fury before departing. The cubs were huddling together up the slope, periodically bobbing up to watch and then dropping down again when the bull gator hissed explosively.

On one pass the panther deliberately appeared to slow down and fairly rolled her body over into a ball to avoid his jaws as they slammed shut inches away. It was an intentional move, a calculated risk exquisitely timed and measured. Before the gator could recharge his posture the cat rolled over and across the top of the great scaly snout. Her hind feet scrambled for purchase in the gator's head and neck as her jaws stretched wide and clamped shut on the end of his nose. His jaws were locked shut. He thrashed, rolled violently and lashed with his tail. But he could neither reach her now nor throw her off. Her hind claws, her vicious rakers and hooks, had found their purchase, had penetrated his thick hide.

They were effectively anchored. The great saurian rolled again and again, battering the cat against the ground. She was bruised and filthy and saliva mixed with muck covered her face. With her forepaws she tore at his throat and chest. She hunched over his face, shrouded him and hugged him in a furiously active embrace. His throat was laid bare and then the bones in his chest, but still she worked at him. In time the alligator died, with the panther, no less furious than when she first saw her cubs endangered, still clinging to his head, still anchored by her rear feet in the back of his neck, still with her forefeet tearing at his throat and chest. At last she kicked herself free and lay on her side, panting desperately. Her hide was ripped and torn, rubbed clear of hair in several places. She had suffered two line fractures in one hip and would limp painfully for several weeks and be limited to only the smallest game. But she had survived and her cubs had survived. They were now wiser as well, for neither of them would ever forget that the waters of the Everglades possess a special kind of hazard and always bear watching.

⚜ 5 ⚜

THERE WAS NO ONE ANIMAL IN ALL OF THE EVERGLADES
that a full-grown panther could not kill, if luck were on its
side. But there were animals that could kill the largest of Florida's panthers, if that was the way the tide of battle went. The
black bear could weigh five hundred pounds and was a killer
in his own right. He alone, of *indigenous* mammals, was a
challenge and he could be a relentless one. Among the reptiles,
of course, the increasingly rare alligator was a danger when
encountered. The even more aggressive crocodiles were further

south and were never seen in the shallow swamps north and inland. The other reptiles of danger were the ground rattler, who could sicken a grown cat and incapacitate it for days; the fiercely aggressive and devastatingly venomous diamondback rattler, whose bite could mean death; the equally aggressive and only slightly less dangerously venomous cottonmouth moccasin and the small, rare and retiring relative of the cobra, the coral snake, whose venom could so deaden an animal's nervous system that its heart would forget to beat. These were the dangerous creatures of the Everglades that the cubs had to learn to handle, these and one more: an exotic species of mammal, an import, a two-hundred-pound primate with a fiercely aggressive disposition, known as *man.*

The areas of Billy Buck Island away from the old Indian village and its feral corn patch appeared from a distance to be an unsoiled, primeval world. The trees were tall, old and original, and were draped with ghostlike festoons of gray moss. In the trees hundreds of ghostlike birds sat and watched the same world they had always watched. The secret pools where alligators and birds nested were silent except for wild voices and were often hung with the kind of watery haze from which dinosaurs once emerged. In the waters around the island, water snakes sculled their timeless S's into the still surface and pushed on out of sight, while greenish-brown gar, holdovers from the Carboniferous period, with bodies so scaled that an axe would rebound, pushed on below in search of prey. All this from a distance seemed to be undisturbed, untouched, perhaps even undiscovered. But such was not the case, not the case at all.

In the waters around Billy Buck Island foreign objects could be found, bobbing for days or weeks and finally coming ashore as flotsam. There were beer cans, expended shotgun shells, expendable soda bottles, plastic debris and all the other signs of the exotic primate that had migrated to this swamp and stayed. Billy Buck was well known to many men and it was rumored among them that there were cats on the island. Still, a mountain lion on his own hunting range is not the sort of trophy the casual hunter takes. He is too sly, too good at keeping secrets, too swift and too sure. He is seldom taken, except by teams of men and teams of dogs.

While the cubs were growing up and learning the pattern of their future lives, men came regularly to Billy Buck and to the waters around its perimeter. There were snipe hunters and the shooters of teal and mallard; there were alligator poachers and boys with .22's ready to shoot anything from bobbing beer cans to black bears. There were occasional older boys with a haunted, pleading look in their eyes and with girls on the verge of decision. There were snake hunters, both professional and amateur, bird watchers, photographers, fishermen, orchid collectors, botanists and even a small archaeological team. They came, they went, and they were often watched. Once or twice the more observant among them noticed the pugmark of a panther and one was keen enough to kneel and examine the area. As he stood he said, "She has cubs with her." It was all right, though, for he was a bird watcher and would not return to shoot. For all its primeval splendor, Billy Buck Island was not a world apart. It was less than forty miles from the towers of Miami Beach, less than twenty minutes' straight run by airboat from Route 41 along the Tamiami Trail. The panther and her cubs were perilously close to civilization and the masses of strangely motivated men who lived there. The miracle, and the importance, of the small family's survival could be measured in no small part by this proximity.

The female panther knew a great deal about men. The most important things she knew about them, really, were that they were dangerous, they should not be hunted or expected to back down in an encounter. This knowledge was ingrained in every fibre of her being and she endeavored on every occasion to pass it along to her cubs. They were beginning to get her urgent message, for she stopped whatever she was doing, even going so far as to abandon a stalk, to retreat into the depths of the hammock every time an airboat snarled by, sending small waves and more bobbing beer cans ashore. Before they were six months old the cubs knew to hiss and spit whenever an airboat was heard, to move into the densest cover available whenever one came close. On the few occasions when humans came ashore and poked around in the brush below the ridge, their mother had hurdled fallen trees and led her cubs on a mad dash to the other end of the island. Once, when the shooting started and ducks began crumpling in the sky, their mother became so unnerved that she crossed the island and led them through the hock-deep water to another island half a mile away, after first scanning the sedge flats. It was their first time off Billy Buck and they were confused and frightened as well as wet when she led them ashore and dodged into a dense thicket to await the silencing of the guns. It came at dusk and under cover of darkness the family of cats returned to their island and to their small and familiar world.

These sudden reactions on the part of their mother taught the cubs what they had to know about man. They adopted her reactions as their own and would carry them throughout their lives. It was the way her mother had learned, and generations of panther mothers before her. Although cats aren't the apparent mimics apes are, example is a most important element in their education. In this case it was all-important, for no panther, no puma anywhere, survives for long when disdainful of man. As a species they can only survive through fear.

On the larger islands, on hammocks where the densest forests grow, the black bear survives. He has been hunted for hundreds of years, but his is a determined species, not easily snuffed out. Although a mite when compared with bears of the North — the polar, brown and grizzly — he is a giant in his world, the largest terrestrial carnivore in tens of thousands of square miles, and very nearly the most short-tempered. Except for a few weeks in the summer when he will take a mate, the black bear is a solitary creature. He will even attack his mate of the year before and drive her away so that he may eat his own cubs. Powerful, cannibalistic, quick to anger, slow to forgive, and always hungry, the black bear was an animal the panther could well afford to avoid.

It was shortly after dawn when the female panther first began to sense that something was wrong. Somehow she had missed the signals during the night but awoke to the awareness, at once infuriating and terrifying, that a black bear had come upon Billy Buck during the dark hours. He weighed four hundred and seventy-five pounds, more than four and a half times as much as the panther. His claws were longer than hers, his jaws as strong. Although he waddled clumsily in girdles of fat, he was laced with muscles and tendons of woven steel beneath and could smash a small cow to the ground with a single blow from either forepaw. He was also very hard to grasp, very hard to hold, because of his size, his heavy coat and robust build. All of this the panther knew by instinct, in the indefinable way of creatures without the power of analysis.

She did not come to her feet when she first sensed the bear's presence but rather held her position low to the ground and began sorting the signals out. He was close and although extremely keen of scent, he had apparently not yet located her and her cubs. If she had been alone an encounter need not have been deadly. A few bluff rushes on his part, accompanied by a lot of roaring and jaw-chopping, and a good measure of hissing and spitting on her part would have been enough. It very often is. All would have quickly returned to quiet as they withdrew to opposite ends of the island to sulk and take their distemper out on smaller animals. Each would have found a displacement activity and one or the other, perhaps even both, would have withdrawn from the island and gone elsewhere. But with young cubs by her side, the panther was a committed avenger. Her fury was apt to surge beyond all bounds and anything she felt was a threat to them she would fight to the death, even when not necessary. Not all female panthers do this, but many are that devoted. The bear, however, was not an imagined threat but a real one. Although he came ashore on Billy Buck in search of birds' eggs, wild fruit, indian pumpkins and termites, he would as happily have eaten panther, young or old. It was while he was slapping frogs to ground that he first got the panther family's scent. He froze in midstroke and allowed a frog to streak to safety as he rose slowly to his hind legs, grumbling, sniffing and squinting his inadequate eyes against the gloom of the thicket at dawn. Pools of saliva collected at the corners of his mouth and he rotated his neck, nose high. The female panther sensed that he had changed his position and heard the increase in his snuffling. In an instant she made her decision. There was to be no contest and with a warning whine she shot over a fallen log and streaked through the brush with her cubs at her heel. Behind her the bear moaned and then wailed his anger and his greed.

In great bounds she cleared the old indian-corn field where she had taken the wild pig before her cubs were born, crashed across the fallen thatch in the Seminole village and turned north to leave Billy Buck on a parallel track with the north-south slough, only east of it where the water was never more than six or eight inches deep. She cleared the shore just a few yards from where the slough dropped down into a deep channel. Her male cub was almost on top of her. The female was almost as quick, but before she hit the water a roar shattered the morning and spun the panther in her tracks.

In great galomping bounds the black bear was rounding the northern tip of the island, splashing through the shallow water, sending up a veil of silvery spray that sparkled briefly in the new light and almost obscured him. Soaked with the spray he created, with his shaggy sides vibrating like great bowls of black jelly, the bear charged. His mouth fell open and between violent choppings of his jaws there issued a wailing, moaning garble of intent.

The panther whined in a rising pitch until her hiss was at least part scream and charged to meet the bear. She was quick but not quite quick enough. The female cub lay dead in the water, her back neatly broken in two. The male cub was just reaching cover back on the shore when the panther made her leap. Her forepaw caught the half-standing bear on the face and exposed all the teeth on his left side, but that was as close as she came. A blow from his right forepaw spun her off into space and she crashed into the water nearly ten feet away, facing in the wrong direction. Her first strike had been damaging to the bear, but his was nearly fatal to her. She was stunned, too stunned for the moment almost to move. But he followed his blow with an immediate charge, ignoring the damage she had done to his face. In two strides he was on top of her. But here she was the more adept. If he was hard to grasp because of his bulk, she was almost impossible to pin because she never was where she appeared to be.

When the bear brought his jaws forward to end the panther's life he had only saw grass and mud to punish. She was out, around and already airborne. Before he could turn she was on his back. Her frantically working forepaws quickly removed one of his ears and his opposite eye. Her hind claws were opening great holes in the flesh along his flanks and her teeth were searching for a hold on the back of his neck. Before she could effect the fatal bite he somersaulted forward and brought his full weight crashing down on top of her, while she was buried in the soft mud, her face underwater. Struggling insanely, with fantastic energy, she moved out from under the crushing weight and spun away before he could strike out with his forepaw. They faced each other at a distance of twenty feet, each sitting back on his haunches and panting for air. His face was mutilated almost beyond recognition and he held his nose high, snuffling and tasting his own blood. Several times he brought his forepaw up and wiped it across his face as if he could erase the damage. She sat watching.

The bear's initial blow to her side and his falling back on top of her with his full weight had not left the panther unharmed. The line fractures she had received in her battle with the bull alligator had never knitted really well and now her left hind leg was all but immobilized. Two ribs had caved in from the bear's first blow and his weight on top of her had driven a broken end out through her flesh. She was bleeding and suffering intense pain with every breath. But still she was ready to fight him, and he her. Something wild, something fierce, something really terrible, had been released in their encounter. Neither was now in command, neither responsible for his own actions. As it had been along the alligator's shore, this was a time and place for death.

Whether or not she caught the sight or scent of her female cub's carcass half submerged near a tuft of saw grass or whether she heard her male cub whimper off in cover beyond the shore, it was the panther that chose to reengage the battle. She rose, still panting, and spit like an exploding boiler as she maneuvered for position, her left hind leg partially dragging. The bear stood on signal and chopped his jaws in return warning and then they both charged at the same time. They came together with a crash, she flailing with her forepaws, all ten claws devastatingly bared. She slashed faster than the eye could follow, but he pressed through, snapping at her, and then rolled his body and struck with his forepaw. The blow that struck her was glancing and she recovered and pressed in again. Three times they came together and pulled apart. He was trying to pin her and she was trying for his neck. His throat was too dangerous, too close to the raking claws on his powerful forefeet.

On the fourth headlong charge he missed with his swiping blow and she was on him, bunched up on his shoulders like a pulsing brown hump that had somehow grown there. He couldn't shake her, although he spun and twisted. Before he could repeat his earlier maneuver and roll over on top of her, burying her in the water that had now been churned into a soup of mud, he stopped. A strange look came into his one remaining eye and his lower jaw sagged. He stood there for an instant and then said, almost exactly in a human voice, "Oh!" It seemed as if he stood there for several seconds, but it was only an illusion, for he was dead and she was disengaging her teeth from the bones in his neck. She had severed his spinal cord after hooking his snout in her forepaws and bending his chin to his chest and he had died quickly, instantly perhaps, and was surprised enough to say, "Oh!," but only once.

🌿 6 🌿

THE PANTHER ABANDONED THE CARCASS OF THE BEAR AND that of her female cub where they lay. She had not killed the bear for food and there was no ritual to be performed over the dead of her own kind. She limped ashore and moved painfully into the thick growth below the ridge with her still terrified male cub tagging behind. There was a shortcut to her old den site along a fallen tree trunk. She took it to avoid moving around the extremely dense growth there but nearly fell several times, as she had trouble keeping her injured hindquarters on the narrow bridge.

She finally reached the den and grunted in pain as her cub pushed on ahead of her. As gingerly as she could, she let her rear end sink down to the ground and with stiffened forelegs adjusted her position before stretching out. Slowly her yellow eyes closed and she slept, this cat the Seminoles called *pa-hay-o-kee,* this cat to whom some tribes had built shrines and most had built legends. She had won again and saved one of her cubs. It was enough.

It was several days before the panther left the old den. Her cub was frantic with hunger and several times each day cried to nurse at her now milkless nipples. Each time she drove him off and he huddled nearby, whimpering. Twice he left the den but quickly returned without having found food. In the midst of plenty he would starve without her, for he wasn't ready to survive on his own. Her death would have been followed by his in a matter of days.

When she did take to hunting again, it was for frogs, nestling birds and hairless rabbits and mice in their bowers of fur and down. He followed behind and imitated her actions and soon he was taking frogs as well. They went together to the southern end of the island where they had rarely gone before and raided nests around the Anhinga pool. Many of the water-turkey nests were far too high for either cat to attempt, but some were low. On one occasion the mother panther managed to pounce on a half-grown female raccoon who had also come to raid the nests and from this treasure she allowed her cub to feed.

It was a bad time for both cats. The mother was always

hungry herself and her temper was short. She was still in pain, and meticulous as she was, worked constantly at the annoyance of a shred of protruding bone on her side. The hole was not knitting well and the infection that had begun there almost immediately after the injury was still festering five weeks later. The cub missed his littermate, not in an emotional way as a human might have done but in another, perhaps as profound. His littermate had belonged in the family unit. She had always been there and he had received the greater part of his education at her side. The play they had engaged in together was a part of that education and something he had thoroughly enjoyed. Also, there was less food now, at a time when he needed more. His mother's shortened temper reflected in his own and he had taken to spitting and hissing back at her. They were two disagreeable cats. Her chances of survival would have been better if she had not had to worry about her remaining cub. His were nil without her. Still they remained together, for that was the plan; it always had been.

In time the panther's injuries did repair themselves. However, she was a much more cautious cat than she had been before. She left Billy Buck Island for three full weeks when a black bear sow came ashore with two cubs of her own. Normally she would have accepted the challenge, perhaps even have hunted the cubs, but now she was more cautious. Her survival and that of her cub depended not on her brute strength but on her cunning, her stealth and her ability to conserve her energy. Somehow she understood this and refused all challenges which she could possibly avoid.

When she finally took again to hunting larger prey, the white-tailed deer and wild pigs in the area, she did so more from ambush than as a stalker. She waited and took them with as short a charge as possible. She no longer enjoyed the chase; she was no longer exhilarated by a contest. The fun had gone out of it. She was anxious to kill as swiftly as possible, to get the prey's muzzle bent back and her teeth into its skull or neck as quickly as she could. From close in she struck often, going to ground on top of prey hit with all her might, and raked with claws like eighteen sabres wielded by as many men. Her prey was quickly downed and killed and her cub thrived and the months from his birth soon numbered twelve.

At a year he weighed just slightly over seventy pounds. His spots were gone along with the rings on his tail, which was now long, cylindrical and as elegant as his mother's. There was no doubt about what he was or about what he was soon to become. He was powerful, more sure of himself every day, and although not quite ready to leave his mother's care, completely a hunting cat. He sharpened his claws on trees and logs several times a day and seemed to enjoy the tugging, the tension it placed upon them and their mechanism. He had learned to drift toward his prey like a billow of tawny smoke and he had learned to kill raccoons, opossum, marsh rabbits and cottontails as well as water rats and smaller rodents. Once he managed to take a gray fox, but he was driven off by an infuriated chittering otter when he sought to take one of her young.

His first real fight was a bitter one, and one from which he learned a number of lessons in technique. While his mother was stalking a white-tailed doe, he happened upon a full-grown bobcat simultaneously stalking the doe's fawn, which had been left hiding in some deep grass. Reacting more than responding, he charged the bobcat, which treed immediately.

The smaller cat stood arched in fury on a heavy limb, staring down at the young panther with all the hate it could muster. Not content with the situation, for he could have taken the fawn, he leaped onto the trunk and started up after the bobcat. Had he been fully grown, and the bobcat was quite able to judge that he was not, the smaller feline would have climbed higher or gone out over his head, hit the ground in a dead run and streaked away to probable safety. But he wasn't fully grown and life was yet full of lessons to be learned. Going up is of necessity somewhat slower than coming down and while going up the young panther met the bobcat aimed in the other direction. It was an angry bobcat, too, for not only had its stalk been spoiled, but its life had been threatened. The bobcat got away neatly, but it was nearly four weeks before the wounds on the young panther's head and shoulders healed. It was the kind of lesson he had to learn, for it was the kind of life he was designed to live.

He was fifteen months old before he took his first deer and the yearling buck did not die neatly. His mother watched from atop a windfall nearby and came down to feed after the severely mutilated animal finally expired. It is ironic but true that a lucky animal is one grabbed by a large and skilled lion, an unlucky one by a near-cub. The latter offers the worse death by far.

With his taking of a deer, however badly it was done, the young panther, for he was now that, had come as far as his mother could bring him. He would one day be a much better hunter than he was then, but that would come from experience, from surviving where death was the easier course, not from anything that could now be taught to him. He was nearly as large as his mother, for she had lost weight after the battle with the bear, and he was eating more food. They occasionally shared a large kill, but more often each took whatever prey he needed for himself. She was no longer grooming him regularly and they were beginning to sleep further apart, meeting almost accidentally when it was time to hunt again. Sometimes they each went off on their own, coming together again only after they had both hunted and fed.

There were still some moments of softness, however, moments that could even be characterized as tender. He would flop down near her and slap playfully at her tail while she rasped her incredibly rough tongue through his hair. She would, at times, wash his face for ten and fifteen minutes while he posed, eyes closed, purring softly. Then he would gently bite her on the throat and she would kick with all four feet, pushing him playfully away. There were these times, but they were becoming more the exception. It was now a matter of convenience that they stayed together at all and the convenience of it was becoming more and more difficult to substantiate in either of their lives.

The rift came just after he passed eighteen months. He was stalking a deer, a careless doe that was feeding far too close to extremely dense cover without checking often for danger. The young male panther was making an unorthodox frontal approach and was just about to smash forward onto the deer in an effort to snap her head back and crack her neck, when his mother burst out from behind the unsuspecting doe and had her head pinned and her skull bitten through before her offspring could move. Then he swung into action. In a spitting challenging fury he came forward to where his mother stood over the carcass, panting. His ears were laid back and he seemed about to strike out at her, when she charged off the deer and sent him flying off into the bushes, lashing out at his rump as he barely pulled away from her. He didn't dare try to join her at the kill and she ate noisily, growling and snarling as she tore into her prey and gorged herself. Only after she had cleaned herself and raked some leaves over the deer's front end did he dare appear sulkily at the clearing's edge. As he did she spit violently at him, laid her ears back and spit again. It was ten minutes after she moved off and disappeared into the bushes before he dared approach her kill. That night they slept nearly half a mile apart.

Men who have known the panther well have said that he is a nocturnal beast, while others equally familiar with the great cat have told of daylight hunts witnessed well and recorded. In fact, just as he is a twelve-month-a-year breeder, he is a twenty-four-hour-a-day hunter. Near man, or when man comes near, he will revert to nighttime hunting exclusively, for he is capable of such almost instantaneous adjustments in the interest of survival. But when he has his range to himself he will hunt when the mood strikes him. On Billy Buck Island, except when their peace was disturbed by the "flying carpets of the Glades" — the airboats with their fumes, their speed and their deafening noise — the panthers hunted by mood and need, not by hour. They were not very active, it is true, when the sun was at its height, but in the morning and in the late afternoon, when it was cooler, they hunted or simply patrolled their range as the fancy took them. Although geared to essentials like reproduction and survival, the panther is not without a measure of capriciousness. He does have moods; he does have fancies.

Now that they had contested a single prey animal and the mother had refused the young panther permission to feed while she was still on the kill, a crack had opened in their relationship that could never heal. In fact, had male panthers been more common in the Everglades, it would have been unlikely that he would be allowed to stay with her as long as he did. She would have driven him off as soon as the opportunity to breed again had presented itself, but that opportunity could only come when a mature male, one at least between two and three years old, presented himself to her. If it had happened when he was still quite young, the male panther could have starved or come close to starving. Elsewhere young panthers have been found abandoned when less than fifty pounds. In cases where panthers have been known to attack men, they were almost always either rabid or very young, early abandoned and near death from starvation. This young panther was fortunate. He was able to stay with his mother until after he could take deer, the biggest item in his diet. He would not starve, nor need he in desperation do anything as wildly foolish as attack a man.

But that time had come. On each occasion when they hunted, her reaction was the same. There was anger and there was the threat of attack. Quite possibly, if he had been a year or so older, she would have accepted him as a mate, but that was not to be. By the time he was old enough to breed, his mother would be a trophy on the wall of a small house in the center of Coral Gables. A month after the young panther left Billy Buck Island in search of a world of his own, five airboats came roaring up the slough from a launching ramp beside the Tamiami Trail. Two were stationed at the north end of the island, three at the south. It was on the southern end, not far from a southward-extending finger of the Anhinga pool, that the dogs were put ashore. They had to travel half-way along the ridge, nearly half a mile, before they picked up her trail. With the pack behind her the panther had to choose between breaking out across the sedge flats or treeing. She chose the latter course and less than fifty feet from where the old Seminole corn patch began, she took a 200-grain soft-point 8mm. Mannlicher-Schoenauer behind the left shoulder at two thousand feet per second and died spitting and kicking as she was blown off the branch by the force of the impact.

🌿 7 🌿

IT WAS A TIME OF WANDERING FOR PANTHER, A TIME FOR
learning and a time for growing. He did not know the fate of
his mother and would have neither understood nor cared had
he known, so Billy Buck Island was behind him as just another
cat's hunting range. He was out to seek one for himself. There
was no panther population pressure to make competition keen
for the hammocks, but there were other factors and even
though he was not yet two years old he understood them, in
that strange way that cats understand the world around them.

Panther needed a fairly large hammock where there were dense places to which he could retreat. He needed an island in the six-inch-deep sea where deer came, where there were birds to attract raccoons and where men did not live or come too often. He needed an island where no other, larger panthers had established ranges, one outside the regular range of any black bears in the area. These seem, perhaps, small enough demands to make of nearly a million and a half acres of Everglades, but it took, in fact, considerable searching; so Panther wandered. He killed as he went, but unspectacularly, wild animals only, and did not come to the attention of human beings. He was at that ideal time of his life when no man knew he was alive. He was still a ghost, a night shadow, and the only tracks he left were upon the mist and upon the water. The hands of the clock wiped his record clean and as a secret animal he was free to live and go his secret ways.

By night he moved across the open flats; by day he examined in detail each new hunting ground he encountered. Many were small, mere specks on the maps of the region, many too small for even that. The names of these pocket wildernesses, those that have names, are sometimes revealing but more often only intriguing. He touched on Rabbit Island, Gopher and Snake, Pumpkin Key, Lostman's Hammock, Willy Willy Island, Dead Sheriff and Indian Camp. Hangman Island is small, Chickee is a little larger and there are Snipe, Gator Island, Six Virgins, Canoe, Dead Dog and Filthy as well. It is a world that has seen many men, many flags and several wars. The men, like the wars, flashed briefly beneath their standards and faded out. They left their debris, they left their unbelievably filthy middens, but they are gone now and Panther wandered at will, hunting, searching, avoiding trouble he was just smart enough to understand he couldn't handle. He was looking for the center of his universe, that point around which he would orbit, and he was in no hurry. There were food and shelter everywhere he went. He was not pursued either by man or the relentlessness of his own sexuality, which had not yet been born. Insofar as a wild predator can be, Panther was at peace. His killing was not a part of war but simple, clean acts of necessity. The animals that died between his jaws or were stunned into oblivion by the hammerblow of his right paw had been designed for that, had been created by nature as surplus to be prey for those who would come along and need them. There was no cruelty in his life, for he had learned how to hunt. He killed what he needed, he was done with games and almost always he killed cleanly and well.

The time had to come, of course, when Panther would give the secret of his existence away. In a world where men have guns that is, unfortunately, the greatest secret an animal possesses. To reveal it is to invite disaster. One warm and humid morning, when the peripatetic wading birds were wondering about the weather, Panther told his secret.

The old man knelt and spanned his fingers across the track. Male, he mused, about two, I reckon. And he looked up, the old man, and squinted out across the flats. *He'll hit Lameduck Island that way. Nothing to keep him there. He'll head on after a day or two, toward Bitterroot.*

The old man knew. He knew all about panthers, for he had hunted them for forty-five years and killed over two hundred. He knew that tracks, that small solitary tracks, probably meant a young cat newly off from its mother, seeking a hammock of its own. Bitterroot would hold the cat, he knew, because there were no cats there at present and no bears to drive a young panther away. He made a mental note. All things being equal, Bitterroot would be huntable in about two years' time. There would be a fair-sized male panther there then, at least for a number of months of the year.

The old man was of less certain lineage than the panther he planned one day to slay. As far as he could figure, he had some Greek ancestry from the old settlement of sponge divers at Tarpon Springs and some French from the turtle fishermen down in Key West. There was some Cuban in him, too, he knew, because at least one of his forebears had worked at Key West in Ybar's cigar factory. There was probably English blood on her side, his mother had once told him, from the cockney English settlers, the Conchs, who had brought their strange accent to the peninsula in the late 1700's. It would not have surprised anyone to find some German back there, too, from the salvage wreckers who had worked the coast years before. His father had once made a joke about his mother's Seminole blood, but he was drunk then and she had gotten very, very angry and advised her son to pay the old man "no mind." That's the way it is with the old people from southern Florida. No one seems to know or care very much about who came from where. Of course, Indian blood doesn't help very much, nor African, although there is a great deal more of both around than most old-timers are willing to admit.

Bitterroot was indeed an island that could hold a cat. It was larger than Billy Buck, nearly half a mile wide at the southern end and a little over a quarter of a mile in breadth in the north. Discounting a narrow projecting finger in the northeast corner nearly two hundred yards long, the bulk of the island was a mile and a half in length. Like Billy Buck, it sat just to the east of a narrow slough which was in places as much as twelve feet deep. A T-shaped ridge began with its cross member spanning the wider part of the island in the south, from there running north for about a mile and a quarter. It then flattened out into a low marshy area as dense as a Brazilian rain forest. In the northwest the slough ran by on its north-south track slightly offshore, but in the southwest it brushed against the island's bulging shore. From this deep area just offshore a number of channels ran and twelve deep pools of random shape, back from the shore and well hidden from the outside world, provided nesting sites and havens for a complex variety of wildlife. It was a wild place and the wonder of it was its closeness to a number of Florida's major cities while it yet retained its character of another time, one presumably long since gone. Like so much of the Everglades, Bitterroot was part of a truly primeval world.

Men had known Bitterroot in the past. Nearly two thousand years ago a band of Tequesta Indians settled below the ridge in the southern end and collected birds' eggs there and hunted deer. They were invaded by, but finally repulsed, a marauding band of Calusas, but not until seven of their own best men were dead. They abandoned the island after that and it remained apart from human events for nearly three hundred years. It was then that Cha-a-na-ra-tee, the ancient and bilious leader of a splinter group of Timucan Indians in northern Florida, sent an expedition into the south to see what was there for them. The warrior that was leading the expedition, Ta-ra-ta-na, succumbed to a rattlesnake bite received on Bitterroot the very day they landed there and the expedition headed back toward the north. Only three of the original eleven men ever made it back at all and Cha-a-na-ra-tee, a less than gentle soul at any time, had them put to death. It was never quite clear to their families why they had to die, but that wasn't a time in history when leaders had to explain themselves, particularly to the kin of executed men.

By the time fourteen hundred more years had passed, the fate of the Glades Indians, to which the Calusas and Tequestas belonged, was sealed. Raiding bands of Creek Indians retreating before the onslaught of the whites in the north were moving south. Later to become known to white settlers as Seminoles, these Creeks were too highly organized for the loosely confederated Calusas, who had themselves long since ridden roughshod over, and submerged, the Tequestas. The Calusas were driven further and further inland away from the desirable lands along the coast and a band settled on Bitterroot. The Calusas had known the Everglades, of course, had explored its reaches by canoe. But few settlements had been attempted and those were temporary. Now a small band of thirty-seven Calusa men, women and children tried to make Bitterroot their home, but a local Seminole chieftain, his name now lost to us, sent his warriors against the village. The Calusas had their bows and arrows and their *atlatls,* or spear-throwers, but they no longer had their spirit. They died to a man and again Bitterroot was abandoned. From time to time after that Seminoles came there to collect turtles, which abounded, and to hunt near the twelve pools along the southwest shore. It was a rich land and one well known to the newly dominant tribe from the north. But in no sense was it an inhabited island.

Shortly after the beginning of the nineteenth century a six-teen-year-old boy by the name of Sammy Goodbody killed his best friend in an argument, the subject of which has never been recorded, and escaped the law by hiding out on Bitterroot Island. When he was about eighteen years old the illiterate youth canoed over to a settlement on the Shark River and in the dead of night "took hisself a cracker girl" of fourteen years old, carried her back to his island and told her she was then his wife.

Sammy's whereabouts remained a secret for nearly thirty years, until 1831, when two deer hunters who had announced their intention of heading out Bitterroot way to try their luck failed to return. Two brothers of one of the men who went out to search for them also vanished. Twelve men finally mounted a consolidated search party and found the four missing men hanging from a tree by their ankles. They had been beheaded. The men located Sammy, by then a gross giant of over three hundred pounds, and hanged him from the same tree where he had tortured and killed the innocent men. The first three ropes they used broke. The fourth held. The girl that Sammy had made his wife was quite mad when they found her huddled nude in a dark corner of Sammy's unspeakably filthy hut and they had to use considerable force to get her into one of their boats. One of the men was badly bitten by her in the struggle and later had to have his hand amputated and very nearly lost the rest of his arm as well, from blood poisoning. It was ru-mored that her teeth were so sharp and her bite so bad because she and Sammy had eaten the children she regularly bore him. The girl, who was then not yet forty-five, but who looked like seventy, died six months after being taken off the island from an unspecified "ailurment." Sammy and his child bride, whose name to this day has never been discovered, were the last full-time settlers on Bitterroot Island. From the very early 1900's on, small cabins were built for weekend use by duck and deer hunters, but they can't be considered settlements as such. Bitterroot, when Panther arrived, was a well known but uninhabited island.

✿ 8 ✿

TURTLES ABOUNDED ON BITTERROOT, THOUSANDS OF THEM, and Panther found these easy to tear apart and eat. On one occasion, as he tore into some debris in which he thought a turtle was hiding, he heard an angry *whirrrr* and flew backward almost too late, just in time to avoid the strike of a badly irritated diamondback rattler who was escaping the midday heat.

There were very few alligators in the island's waters, for the poachers had been there many times. Those few that were left were small and not likely to survive the attrition natural to the area. There were other amphibious creatures, though, uncountable thousands of frogs and toads, at least nine kinds of turtles, and snakes of which more kinds were harmless than dangerous. All of the small mammals that had been found on Billy Buck were on Bitterroot as well, only more of them because of the island's larger size. It would have been all but impossible for even a less experienced animal than Panther to have starved and he settled down to check the hammock out in detail. There were deer on the north end of the island, more or less permanent residents, and several areas where raccoons were in plentiful supply. There were tens of thousands of crayfish to be found in the waters around the hammock and in its pools, and upon these the small hunters thrived. There were skunks on the island, too, and in a pinch these could be taken with a little special care. There were no permanent wild-pig residents, but signs abounded to prove that they came there regularly. The hammock was one of the very few areas within the Everglades where the nine-banded armadillo had become established. Probably descended from imports brought eastward from Louisiana by men with some purpose or other in mind, these small armored mammals managed to get a substantial foothold in a number of areas on the peninsula. Bitterroot, for better or for worse, was one of these, and armadillo holes were everywhere to be found.

As might be expected of so rich a larder, bears were not unknown to the island. However, the island had been hunted so often and bears so frequently taken in the preceding decades that those that had survived had a bad memory of the place and generally stayed away. But there were always old tramp bears moving through that part of the Glades, big old bears beyond their prime and filled with resentment, and they found Bitterroot and stopped there often enough to bring back an occasional bear hunter for a "look-see an' a sniff a' the old place."

Because of its great size and the way in which it loomed up out of the flats, because it sat hard by a major north-south slough carrying water from Okeechobee to the sea, and because the dense thickets that crowded its beaches promised safety to many a threatened animal, panthers included, Bitterroot had a highly mobile transient population. In fact it was a crossroads. On the one hand, that was good for the hunter — a varied diet was always available — and on the other hand, bad. Other predators knew about the hammock as well and more than one bear, more than one panther, had died there in violent battles and had sometimes been eaten. The numbers of both species shot and skinned could not even be reckoned. Just as many had been shot and allowed to crawl away to die. At best, the hammock known as Bitterroot Island was a dangerous and violent place. But then, to all of the natural inhabitants of the Everglades, Panther was a dangerous and violent animal. He and Bitterroot Island suited each other.

The world of the Everglades has two seasons, not four. The average summer temperature varies from the winter by only eighteen degrees. Monthly precipitation, however, varies from 1.4 to 9 inches. The two real seasons are the *wet* and the *dry*.

It was November, the dry time, a time of danger in a world where water is the fulcrum of the natural balance. In the shallowest places out on the flats, dry ground was showing and the smaller pools no longer fed by either surface water from the north or by precipitation were drying out. Fish were dying by the thousands and so were frogs and turtles.

Ironically, those smaller aquatic and semi-aquatic animals that did survive would do so in many cases because of the alligator. It had dug many a hollow in the mud and here available water collected and life lasted longer. The alligators that had survived the poachers gathered at ever smaller pools and here the wading birds accumulated as well. It was stark, sere, a bad time.

The slough west of Bitterroot still had water, but it was markedly less than in the other season and steep banks showed that had been completely submerged when Panther first found the island. Of course, there was water to drink, for the hammock had pools and small ponds that survived the drought. The water wasn't as sweet and the number of snakes that gathered near this supply was dangerously high. It was now that Panther, in a single careless moment, was struck in the left foreleg by an eighteen-inch ground rattler.

When the snake struck, Panther flew straight up in the air as if his legs had been coiled springs. The pain was immediate and grew rapidly in intensity. The snake, one of dozens in the immediate area, had struck out from behind a small pile of debris as Panther stepped across it and had caught the careless cat just above the elbow. Luckily, a blood vessel had not been hit, but well-blooded muscle tissue was involved.

A very sick cat crawled away into a sheltered nest he had found beneath a windfall, a nest where a now dead panther mother had once raised her young, and lay there for several days. He shifted his position constantly in an effort to find a way of alleviating the pain. In four days a very hungry cat was limping out to hunt again, but it would be months before his leg would heal. He was lucky to have survived not only the envenomation but the secondary infection that followed.

In the few days that Panther was incapacitated by the bite of the small rattler, things had deteriorated even further in the world of the Everglades. No rain had fallen anywhere on the entire peninsula of Florida or on any of its islands in several weeks. The spillage from Lake Okeechobee had all but stopped completely and the groundwater that remained was fast disappearing. There was a constant, a discernibly frantic movement among the animals of the area. The otters were all gone, gone to where there were still flowing rivers where they could survive. The birds that depended on aquatic life had also moved away for the most part or had gathered along the drainage ditches that men had built and that had helped endanger the area by carrying off too much water in a way that did no one any good.

Then it started, over to the west, but how, no one will ever know. At first there was only a hint of a black thread drifting up and away into a cloudless sky, but then there was another and another. In a matter of minutes there was a cluster of black smoke bunched up to the southwest, then another to the northwest. In less than half an hour they were joined and the light was changing its value. A full-blown saw-grass fire was underway and moving across the Glades of its own free will. There had been no wind at first, but now there was, a wind that carried the stink of the fire with it because it was fire-born, fire-bred and fire-reinforced.

Panther had never smelled fire before, but like all living

creatures who may ever face the possibility of smoke and flame, he had an instinctive dread of its scent. At the first hint of it in the wind, he raised his head and stared off toward the west. He moved down to the shore as the first flights of ducks hammered frantically overhead. As it grew darker, as the fire moved closer, the birds increased in number and variety. Egrets that had not yet moved off streamed past. Snipe and smaller birds, many of them newly arrived visitors from the north, bunched up overhead, exploded into ever changing patterns, reconsolidated into tight flocks and burst outward again as they pulsed their way across the sky.

Panther was distracted for a moment when the first deer streamed into view, their dainty little hooves beating a distinctive tattoo on dry land where only weeks before water had flowed. There were two deer, then two more, then six, then ten. Dark little humps out on the flats moving toward Bitterroot took shape. There were raccoons, skunks, rats of all kinds and grizzled opossums. They were moving toward Bitterroot, around it, and on the eastward side of the island, fire-wise survivors of other droughts were moving off the island and away.

Now, from where Panther stood, a bright red-orange line could be seen below the black pall that all but filled the sky. There was a new noise, too, a *whoooosh* that seemed to promise that it would soon become a roar. The flames could be seen clearly and sparks and bits of burning matter were being carried on the wind. In the trees overhead these small incendiaries were being caught in the Spanish moss and clumps of it were beginning to smolder. Panther turned and fled to the hammock's interior, for he was no less panicked than all of the other animals. Here was a threat against which there was no counterthreat. Here a blow of the paw could gain him nothing; there was no purchase for his claws in the fire winds.

The fire, only minutes old, had already consumed millions of lives, billions upon billions, really, if the insects were included. Small pools had been sucked dry in seconds as the fire passed overhead. With a sizzling, snapping sound, water vanished and the mud curled and cracked and turned ash-gray. Birds rising late from grassy hides were snatched up by the heat and smashed to the ground, where they kicked convulsively for a second or two, no more. Fish stared upward in disbelief as the heat stripped their cover of water away and filled their gills with soot. They kissed the wind with foolishly puckered mouths for an instant and began to cook. Snakes coiled convulsively by the thousands, for they had neither the legs nor the wings that could carry them away from danger. All across the seared landscape they could be seen thrusting their coils in loops to the sky in the grotesque postures of the dead and the damned. Turtles, slower yet, baked in their own ovens.

The heat was suffocating on the hammock, and oxygen needed to support the flames that now were moving across the flats like a flood, was being drawn from the air, making it poorer and less sustaining. The noise was now incredible, and the stink sickened the cat and all the other creatures that had remained on the island. Streams of fire had flowed past the hammock on the south and a freshet from the south had pushed these fingers of fire toward the north. Animals that had fled from Bitterroot were being killed where they were caught in the open. Few even managed to cry out; they just curled and contorted and cooked. Thousands upon thousands of crayfish had already been boiled and abandoned; millions of frogs and toads had had their skin blister before their bodies popped and spilled out onto the ashes to become in the ensuing seconds little but ash themselves.

Only minutes remained before Panther would lose consciousness and his hide would begin to steam. He had waited too long. He didn't have the strength to flee and the air didn't have the oxygen left to help him muster any last bit of energy. On the westward shore three ancient docks that hunters had made for their punts had already passed the steaming point. The moisture that had gathered there for generations was gone and the wood, now like paper, would turn to flame in another minute or two with a slight explosive sound. In fact, there were a thousand places where the island was ready to burst into flames. The last moisture from its leaves, the last sap from its trunks, the last drops of water from the humus underfoot, were evaporating. In minutes all of the hammock, all of Panther's new world, would vanish.

Since fires were blazing independently of each other in a hundred different places in Florida at that moment and since rain had to fall in each of these places eventually, and since it had to start somewhere, it would be stretching a point to say that the cloudburst was a miracle. It was one, perhaps, for Panther, because it saved his life, and seven of his kind had already died in fires that day.

At any rate, the rain fell.

It came in torrents; it came from clouds too masked by soot and smoke to be seen. Fire speck after fire speck sizzled out of existence and a billion places saw ash and fire dust pocked by drops in the first seconds. In ten minutes the fire was out and small flowing streams were beginning to wash the dead into the sloughs that would float them away toward the Gulf.

With the water came a drop in temperature and with the wind came air and life. Panther and millions of other creatures that had survived limped off to rest and just to breathe. They now carried the seed for those that had perished. They now carried the past, and the future. Water and wind, air and life, flowed across the scarred land and repaired it and called down to those that still panted in the steaming destruction to repair themselves as well, because after the fire, as after all things that come and go in the lives of the wild, there is life, there is life, and that is all there is, all there ever was.

🌿 9 🌿

AS A NEARLY MATURE CAT PANTHER WAS NOW THE
personification of grace. His coat did not resist moisture so he
stayed on high ground as much as possible, taking to water
only when really necessary. But when on dry ground, his
movement was fluid, an effortless flowing forward or leaping
up. With his low-hanging belly swinging from side to side, he
seemed to move from one place to another without conscious
effort, without even being aware that an effort was being expended.

Very swift prey could escape him if they could stay clear of his claws. He could for brief spurts reach thirty miles an hour, but he didn't have the stamina to hold at that speed. He depended on other skills to keep himself fed. There were his superb muscular coordination, his soft cushioned feet and his skill at concealment — these were the factors that made him successful and made the deer's speed of little avail when Panther began his stalk. There was the sudden preliminary movement that might alert the deer, but almost always too late to help it; the spring, the strike with claws extended and the awful sound of body against body. Panther's claws were so constructed that the harder his prey struggled, the deeper they set. Then came the sigh, and Panther's railing breath as it whistled out of the corners of his mouth, slipping past the death grip he held on his prey.

Although he made soft snarling and growling sounds while he fed, and often purred as he cleaned himself after eating seven to ten pounds of deer meat at a feeding, he was usually silent. The time would come when he would be somewhat noisier, but that required another cat nearby, another cat with special meanings for him. The combination *mew* and parrot noises he had made as a cub were behind him. The birdcalls and caterwauling he would do as a cat about to mate were in the future. At this point in his life Panther was as solitary and about as silent as he could be.

Silent though he might have been, Panther was not able to keep his existence secret. Wherever he went on Bitterroot — along the shores, near the pools, on high ground near the Indian middens or past the wreckage of the Goodbody hovel

— he left his sign. And the old man came from time to time to check, and he knew he had been right.

"He's growin' up," he would say to himself. *"Gonna be a good size."* You have to look at a lot of panther tracks before you can kill two hundred or more of the cats. And when you look at that many panther tracks, you have to learn something about the animal that made them.

Panther's tracks were clear and unmistakable. They were well defined in moist ground especially, wide and somewhat rounded. His heelprint was lobate, triangular with a somewhat pearlike outline. Only four of the toes on his forefeet printed. The fifth toe, on the inside of his leg, was too high up and was never seen in his track. His claws showed only rarely, when he was slipping down a bank or occasionally when he sought purchase for a spring. When seen separately his hind footprint was narrower than the fore, with the heel pad less pronounced. Otherwise they were very similar. Eventually the individual pawprint he would leave in the mud would be four inches long and nearly five wide. It was still a shade short of that, for Panther still had some growing to do. His paws, however, would reach full size before he would, for they were always in the lead. At six months he had had paws nearly the size they would be at a year.

The legend had started far west of the Everglades and a little to the north, in New Mexico. The Indians there had known the panther as well as the Calusas, the Tequestas and the Seminole-Creeks had. There, where he was called *yutin,* they said he buried his excreta because he knew it would turn into precious jewels and he didn't want man, his archenemy, to have the benefit of them. Actually he had other motives, un-conscious, automatic ones, but to someone who has killed two hundred panthers, his actions could be read like a book.

There were a great many things the old man could tell from the small signs that Panther left that day. He bent over the track so that his shadow would fall on it and accentuate its outlines. Panther's age was immediately apparent. His toes were still rounded, not elongated as they would become with age. They were tucked in close to the heel pad, making a com-pact print. As he aged, his foot would splay out, but there was no sign of that as yet. Also, his hind feet registered, fell neatly into the tracks made by the forefeet. With his aging, his hind feet would start lagging behind his forefeet, leaving clearly separate prints. The track also told the old man that Panther's pace had been leisurely. Here again the fact that his tracks registered gave the clue. As a panther's pace increases, his hind feet overshoot his forefeet. The further ahead of the forefeet the hind feet hit, the faster an animal's pace.

There were a number of other things to be read from Pan-ther's unmistakable sign that day as well. The tracks he was reading were fresh, the old man knew, because the ridges be-tween the toes were still moist. Those ridges dry out quickly and the fact that they were as moist as they were meant that the tracks were little more than minutes old. The old man felt a tingling sensation as he read the signs. He always did when he knew a panther was near. It was why he kept hunting them. It was the thrill, the only thrill left to him, and he couldn't part with it.

In fact, the tracks were very fresh indeed. Panther crouched on a heavy limb forty feet off the ground and studied the old man as the old man studied the tracks. The old man was coming regularly to Bitterroot now and Panther had stopped flying off in terror at the first sign of the small dinghy coming up the slough from the south. He had taken to studying the old man as carefully as the old man had been studying him. They were sizing each other up. For the moment it was a standoff.

On this particular day the old man was following up each lead. He was doing more than just checking to be certain "his" cat was still there on the hammock, which was all he usually did. Cats make their scent posts without relationship to an upright object, unlike male dogs. The male cat makes a very pronounced scrape and from it the old man could identify Panther as a male — a female scrape, when made, is much less pronounced — and also reaffirm his direction of travel. In making his scrape the male cat crouches down in his trail, facing the direction of his travel, and draws a small amount of dirt and debris toward him with one or both paws. When he has a small mound he steps forward and deposits his urine on it and continues moving forward in the same direction. Very often he will leave a single track in the small excavation made by his scrape, but not always. At any time the old man could judge the cat's line of travel by the relationship of the mound to the scrape hole. It was like reading a map.

Before the old man had learned to read animal signs effectively he had had to learn about his animals. He knew the animals of the Glades as few other men alive did because he was different from other hunters in one very important way. He didn't hunt with dogs, which is just about the only way panthers have been hunted in Florida for a century. Men who hunt with dogs, who depend on their hounds' noses to read the only sign they care to know about, seldom learn the exquisite details of the tracker's art. Scrapes, scats, lying-up places and the ridges between the cat's toes are the fine points in a fine art. A man trailing behind six yowling hounds doesn't know they exist. For the old man, a unique remnant of the true woodsman tradition, they were the last links he had with a world that no longer existed. Each cat he tracked and killed "in th' old way" was a new lease on life for an era he could not admit had long been dead. A fairly tracked panther, fairly killed, was the sacrifice the old man laid at an altar where no one else seemed to worship. He was as much an anachronism as the land developers would have us believe the Everglades itself is.

A man who would know his panther must know the very intimate details of his life. The scats alone can tell a tracker as much as a signpost can the uninitiated. Meat eaters' scats are black and weather to white with age. The age of a scat, then, is immediately apparent. The depositing of a scat, of course, must follow a feeding and the number of times the panther has visited his kill can also be judged by the scat. On the first few visits to a medium- or large-sized kill the panther will eat only the most desirable portions: the liver, the blood and the soft muscle tissue. Scats that follow later visits to a cache will show more hair and bits of bone. The nature of the prey can also be judged, of course, by the incompletely digested matter left behind.

Since a panther will rest up, often for several days, after a very large meal, the hunter is benefited by knowing the location of the lying-up places. After lying up, the cat will move off and desposit scats in two or three locations on his line of travel. The deposits will inevitably be of diminishing size.

With patience a skilled tracker can backtrack to where the panther rested. It can be useful knowledge to have for future reference.

And so the old man read the signs that bit by bit fitted together to form the ghostlike outline of the cat we call Panther. He knew with practiced certainty as he stood there, staring off into the gloom of a thicket where Panther had indeed been lying up, that this cat, too, would be his. His tracks and signs were classics of their kind — the kind of things you would hope to find if you had a novice with you and were teaching him the panther's ways.

"Well, Doc Painter," — for that is what he was called and what he called himself, the Painter being a corruption of "Panther" — *"ya got him when ya want him."* And strangely, the words were spoken with affection. Doc Painter had been at it so long that he no longer understood it himself. Indeed, he wouldn't have known what you were talking about if you had explained it to him. He loved panthers, thought them the most beautiful animals alive, yet he killed them, year after year after year. It was no longer sport, not really. He had become too good at it. He moved and thought and acted like a panther himself. He had cracked their code and no panther would ever be likely to escape him. He knew what a panther would do before the panther himself. It was no contest, but the old man couldn't stop doing it. He was indeed the last of his kind — a lion hunter. The death of the great cats — cats he loved and understood far better than he ever had people — was the thing he had always lived for. His was the kind of predation the cats themselves would have found incomprehensible, except when as kittens they used all living things at hand as pawns in the

endless practice sessions we call play. But cats, unlike men, grow up.

Doc Painter didn't want the cat just yet. He knew he still hadn't bred and that would have been a waste. The old man wanted "his" panther's seed firmly planted before he took him. He wanted cats to take in the ensuing years. Doc Painter, like the alligator, was ancient, and he had learned how to wait.

𝕝 10 𝕝

THE TIME HAD COME IN PANTHER'S LIFE FOR HIM TO BREED, for he was nearly three years old. He was a slightly larger than average specimen of his kind, weighing just over one hundred and forty pounds. He measured eight feet ten inches from the end of his broad pinkish nose pad to the tip of his tail. All signs that he had ever been a kitten were gone. He had been completely solitary for over a year and was secretive in everything he did. With the exception of the single occasion when he had come upon panther signs at the extreme northern end

of Bitterroot, signs that another immature male cat was seeking an island of his own, he had not had contact with his own
kind since the day he left Billy Buck and his mother behind.
The young male that had touched briefly at his island had departed within hours. They would probably have fought if they
had met.

But now he was three, or nearly so, and he was ready to
assume a new role in his life. His need was not cyclic, like a
female's, but he did have the urge to wander at least part of
the time and to find receptive mates. The time had not yet
come in history when the last specimen of his kind would
wander through life in the supreme frustration, but mates
were becoming more and more difficult to find. As Doc Painter
knew he would, Panther had to travel.

In fact, within a week after Panther began his wandering,
Doc Painter came to Bitterroot and examined several of "his"
cat's regular trails. When he found no fresh sign he made
plans to come again in a few days. After he failed to locate
fresh signs on the third consecutive visit, he stood staring out
across the flats and whispered to his friend, *"Go, boy, go. I'll
meet ya here in a couple of months' time."*

In his initial swing to the east, Panther came within a mile
of Billy Buck but then swung north and passed the area by.
Whether it was a conscious or instinctive act we cannot say, for
no one can possibly judge what a panther remembers or what
a panther knows. We can only see their actions and try, without projecting ourselves, to judge the motivation there.

On his move to the north Panther came upon a smaller island, a much smaller one, and stayed only long enough to kill
a raccoon and eat from it once. Thirty of the animal's original

thirty-five pounds were left to the insects who were quick to move in.

Further north was a string of smaller islands yet, each no more than a few acres in area. On one Panther killed a deer; on another he tried but failed to take a prize from a small group of wild pigs.

For no particular reason we can discern, Panther began moving west after his abortive pass at the wild pigs and presently found a series of larger hammocks with greater promise.

He had barely come ashore on Mill Island, the first really large island he had encountered since leaving Bitterroot, when a snarling hiss from within the ruins of an old cabin presented the challenge. He flew toward the cabin and then skirted it in time to see a bobcat, a grizzled old male, leap out through a window in the rear and streak away toward a growth of particularly tall trees. Panther was after him and the bobcat treed almost immediately. Panther circled the tree from below, spitting and snarling furiously, while the bobcat put on no less a show on a heavy branch that hung out over his pacing enemy.

The display, the insult and counterinsult, went on for several minutes before Panther turned and moved away from the tree. Then he spun so fast that the carefully watching bobcat took a step backwards on his branch and nearly fell off. Panther spun and hit the tree an incredible eighteen feet above the ground. That was within two feet of where the bobcat stood arched up in fury, his hate fairly bristling, personified in each erect hair. Before the smaller cat could react Panther was on the branch, on him, avoiding his furiously lashing paws, with his teeth firmly planted in the bobcat's neck. His hind claws took their purchase and stretched the smaller cat's body out, strung him away flailing helplessly at the air. With a final spit of hate, with a last venomous comment, the bobcat relaxed and his eyes clouded over. Panther had been on the island for just under ten minutes. The bobcat had been hunting the area for thirteen years.

Panther ate perfunctorily from the bobcat's carcass before setting out to investigate the potential of Mill Island. It was night when he moved away from the woods behind the old cabin and found a trail that moved westward across the island. He wasn't hungry so he didn't accept the challenge and the lure of a buck that bounded away in terror and he ignored a large female raccoon that ambled along a windfall and plopped down into some water beyond. The scents he encountered were rich and varied, for pigs had been there recently and there was more than that single white-tailed buck. But the scent he was seeking was absent and thirty-six hours later, without bothering to feed again, Panther abandoned Mill Island and headed west again.

On two of the islands he came upon in the weeks that followed, he encountered bear smell and left without bothering to investigate further. He wasn't on a warring mission; he was seeking a mate. Several times in his wandering he found panther signs, but they were stale and were either from males or females not in heat when they autographed the wind.

Panther wandered over two hundred miles before he found the first trace of the goal he was seeking. He had wound in and out from hammock to hammock, he had followed slough after slough and had had to swim in deep water a number of times. He had killed along the way and avoided the bigger fights with bears he had sensed and bears he had seen. But now he was close to claiming the missing element in his life. He followed the female's track across several small hammocks until she finally stopped on a long thin island called Snakey, not for any special inhabitants it harbored, but for its shape. It was nearly two miles long and nowhere more than a hundred yards wide. It twisted and hooked from north to south and carried on its spine some of the densest vegetation in the Everglades region. Somewhere within the two-mile-long tangle the female waited while Panther sorted out his instincts, recalled those things his species's history, not his mother, had taught him. But come ashore he did, just at dusk, and stood on the beach, chirping like a bird.

At first even Panther was surprised at the intensity of the sound that issued from the thicket in front of him. It started neither low nor high; it just blossomed out into the dusk and rolled out across the saw-grass flats. *Owww ooooo owww oooooo hurhhhhhhhhh.* It was like the insane scream of a woman in pain, in fear for her life. It was like a boat whistle, like a steam locomotive, like a small mad boy. It was all of these things, all the things the old woodsmen used to say it was, and all the things that drove the early settlers into each other's arms and spun off into rumors of witches and demons in the New World's woods. It was also the sound armchair zoologists in big city museums spent a century claiming didn't exist. It was the mating call of a female panther, one of the most controversial sounds in all of the western hemisphere.

Panther held his ground on the shore and chirped again. The sounds he made were ridiculous in contrast to those of his prospective mate and again she wailed. *Owwww ooooo owwww ooooo hurrrrhhhhhh.* As the second incredible scream echoed out across the flats, Panther started forward toward the ridge in twelve-foot bounds. Before he had gone twenty yards he realized that the lady had not sung for him. Almost too late he saw the big male spring and was barely able to twist his body aside and avoid the full force of the impact. The rival cat was bigger, outweighing Panther by twelve pounds. He also had seven more years of experience behind him and although Panther fought valiantly, he was hopelessly outclassed. By the time he was allowed to slip off Snakey Hammock and move across the half mile of open sedge flats to a smaller island beyond, he had suffered several long, very deep lacerations on his left flank and two on his right shoulder. It was astonishing that the larger, older and wiser cat hadn't bothered to finish him off but for some reason chose to let the smaller intruder go free. Of course, the older panther had a few scratches of his own to attend to. Panther, two days after he turned three years old, found and lost his first female within the space of an hour. Nature had decided that another male was available that had been better proven, whose potential was more certain. Only when a better male was not on hand could Panther breed. That was the scheme.

Panther lay up for several days on the small hammock west of Snakey. He didn't bother to hunt while he was there. On the fourth day — during the night of the fourth day — he headed west again and killed and ate a raccoon hunting crayfish out on the flats. He continued his weaving course, heading toward each piece of high ground as it loomed into view. Ironically, he was only eighteen miles due north of Bitterroot, to the east of the same slough that ran past his own hammock, when he found a receptive female and had her without challenge.

The small panther he mated on the forty-seventh night of his odyssey had been mated once before but had not delivered living cubs. She would not bear Panther's either, for her organs were deformed and she would abort before she was halfway through her gestation period. The fact that her periodicity continued to plague her was a small, quiet irony. For Panther's part of it, it was a complete enough experience. In his eagerness he mated with her seven times before she vanished one day as he rested. He didn't bother to follow her.

In the dead of night following his mate's disappearance, by some unexplainable instinct he headed south and when dawn first began specking the sky in the east, he reached the northern tip of Bitterroot. Less than six hours later Doc Painter came ashore on the southern end and began checking to see if "his" cat had returned.

In the weeks and months during which he bided his time, waiting for Panther to mate and to be ready for the taking, Doc Painter had the beginnings of second thoughts. He was near eighty now, as near as he could figure, and he had killed at least those two hundred panthers. In all that time, he pondered, he had never taken one alive. They belonged to him only after they were dead and even he had to admit that a carcass is not the same thing as a living animal. In fact, since he had never been to a zoo, Doc had never had a chance to study a living panther for any length of time. He had seen them for seconds or minutes at most, always at a distance and never without a rifle in his hands. Slowly the idea built in his mind that he would like to own a panther, to be able to look at one for more than a few fleeting seconds, to come to really *know* the first panther in his life.

Panthers, Doc Painter knew, very often have the peculiar quality of resignation once trapped. They are not apt to thrash around the way other animals do and they won't chew off their own leg to escape. They generally lie quietly and await their fate; no one has ever been able to explain why. The result is that a panther taken in a bear trap or a smaller version of that device is usually less scarred than an animal of another species. Still, the old man didn't want his first panther that way. He wanted him clean, uninjured, uncrippled, for this panther was going to be different. This panther was going to be his pet, his proud possession. Since he knew that "his" cat was already nearly full-grown, the idea was a silly one. What he wanted to accomplish could be done with a kitten taken early from its mother, but never with a fully grown cat. The old man wanted to imprint the panther to make him truly his. He didn't understand the phenomenon in the same way a scientist would have done, but he knew the end result he desired. It was a foolish idea, but Doc Painter was a foolish old man of eighty who had lived alone for sixty-five years and done little or nothing but hunt in all that time.

Whenever he came to Bitterroot to check on Panther's progress, Doc Painter thought a little more about taking his first cat alive. After he ruled out the bear trap, he began casting around for an alternative. Several times he had found Panther's unmistakable tracks leading in and out of an abandoned hunter's cabin on the eastern shore of the hammock. There were many mice and rats that used this shack as they used all others and from time to time, it was apparent, Panther stopped when he was passing and had a small game of pinning a few of the frantically scurrying rodents. The old man could just picture the pandemonium that must have broken loose every time he entered the hut.

Doc Painter examined the roof of the shack and determined that it was solid, that a cat couldn't break through and escape that way. The walls were in good condition, too, except for a couple of spots that could be easily shored up. Three windows would require sealing and a device would have to be fitted to the door that could be tripped to effect the capture.

All the carpentry was done during Panther's absence. The windows had two-by-fours set across them and anchored to the frame of the building with spikes. The few weak spots in the wall were laced with scraps of plywood overlaid with additional two-by-fours, and they were now strong enough to hold. Several places in the floor looked as if they could be torn up by an infuriated cat and extra wood was nailed down in these spots as well. All of the lumber needed was stripped off another cabin a little less than a quarter of a mile away along the hammock's shore.

For the trap itself, the old man fashioned a heavy plank door with a burlap bag full of stones affixed to it to give it weight. A simple pulley led to the inside of the shack and was anchored by a single rope to a shelf four feet off the floor. The shelf was held in place by a few brads, just enough to hold it in place against the strain of the rope that held the door. With any additional strain at all the shelf would tear loose and the door would fall. That was the plan. Sooner or later Panther would come by the cabin and Doc Painter had the means of making him put that needed strain on the shelf and make himself a prisoner within the abandoned hunter's shack.

⚘ 11 ⚘

PANTHER STAYED PRETTY MUCH TO THE CENTRAL RIDGE
after his return to Bitterroot. He was never more than a few-
score yards from one or another of the twelve pools. He came
down off the ridge just at dusk to take some small birds or an
occasional raccoon, wading through six-to-eight-inch-deep
water to do so. As a result, it was over a week before Doc
Painter found unmistakable signs that "his" panther had returned. By that uncanny sixth sense experienced trackers use to
confound the uninitiated, the eighty-year-old man recognized

Panther's footprint the way a less skilled man might have been able to recognize his face, or his whole form.

The old man was too shrewd to make his move until just the right moment. He knew how to play the cat-and-mouse game as well as Panther. In addition, he understood it. It would be at least several weeks, he knew, before Panther would wander again. He had all the time he needed without rushing things. His timing and his anticipation of Panther's movements had been flawless so far. In the contest, as far as it had gone, human intelligence had been the determining factor. However deficient the intelligence of the ancient illiterate might have been, it far, far exceeded that of any cat that had ever lived.

As the old man could have predicted, Panther did not return to Bitterroot the same cat he had been when he began his wandering. His first odyssey had marked him. Each new animal he had killed, each new piece of land he had hunted, had taught him something. And, too, he was now a mated cat. The irony of his having fathered no cubs did not reflect on him at all. He had gone through the motions and he was now a different kind of cat.

Doc Painter was able to detect and perhaps even sense the changes Panther had undergone as soon as he began tracking him. He would find the trail he was following suddenly vanishing from under his nose and he would nod with appreciation. He would smile and look up into the trees overhead. He was seeing "his" cat develop, and he was strangely proud of him. Had he been a younger man, he would have scaled the trees around the end of the trail to find the marks where Panther's claws had fought for purchase. If the old man had climbed a tree or two he would have been likely to find the cat itself crouching low against a heavy branch nearby. Panther was watching Doc Painter and was more than a little interested in the old man's unaccountable behavior. While the human hunter was adept at reading signs, the cat he sought had the sense of smell, the sense of hearing and the ability to conceal himself that gave him the distinct advantage. The cat read the man as often as the man read the cat.

Panther made very few kills that Doc Painter did not soon come to know about. He developed no routines that the old man didn't disrupt by discovering and then, eventually, anticipating. It was becoming a war of nerves and the wise old panther hunter began to suspect that it had gone as far as it should. Any further, he reasoned, *"an' that old panther's gonna up and quit Bitterroot. No sense in pushin' 'im too far."* In a very real sense the relationship a man establishes with a wild animal is like the link he forms with another human being. It is fine, it is critical and it can be easily destroyed. Somehow even the old man understood this, not instinctively but consciously. It had accounted for all the success he had ever known in his life.

For two days the old man stayed away from the hammock, but when he returned on the third he carried a small medicine bottle with a cork stopper. Later that same afternoon Panther came across the first drops of the lure the hunter intended to use as the instrument of his downfall. Only a few drops had been spilled, but Panther caught the scent and moved down to investigate. He located the rag and rolled on it, sniffed it deeply and noisily, and rolled on it several more times. He picked it up in his teeth and carried it off with him, dropping it from time to time to sniff it and roll on it again. Panthers are no less susceptible to oil of catnip than house cats. Of course, their size makes them appear even more absurd.

The scent soon wore off the rag and Panther abandoned it. It was five days before he found a second lure and treated it in much the same way he had the first. This time, though, the lure was a torn doll and it reeked of man-smell. Still, the catnip was strong and after only slight hesitation Panther ignored the man-smell and abandoned himself to his heady drunken games. The doll was all but completely destroyed before Panther finally left the remnants beside the trail and set off to hunt.

Four times Panther was lured; four times he responded without harm befalling him. He had gotten used to the association of the man-smell with that of the catnip lures. He no longer found it particularly disturbing. On the fifth occasion, when he caught the scent as he passed by an abandoned hunter's cabin, he swung toward it without breaking his pace. Coming upon the scent unexpectedly had become something of a habit, which was exactly what the old man intended. Panther's normal guards were down.

The rich and unmistakable man-smell that reeked throughout the cabin's interior did not disturb Panther as he entered, for the oil-of-catnip scent was deeper than he had ever known it before. More had been used and it was inside a fairly closed system of limited air circulation. Panther stood in the twilight of the main room and mewed softly to himself. The scent drifted down to him from a high point in the smaller room beyond. Ignoring several mice that scurried out of his way and the hysterical anger of a land rattler that huddled beneath the floorboards, Panther moved forward to the door that led to the room beyond. The smaller room, like the larger one, and like the grounds that surrounded the cabin, was filthy. Litter and debris, human and animal, but largely human, were everywhere. Cobwebs breached every opening that an insect might use as an avenue. Stalagmitic animal droppings were hardened into place and, slowly surrendering their odors, had whitened with age. To any other creature the rooms whose threshold he spanned would have been rich in a variety of scents, most associated with decay, abandon and the passage of time. To Panther, however, the oil-of-catnip odor overwhelmed all others and after only a moment's hesitation and with a single lash of his tail, he left the floor. The tightening of the muscles in his hind legs was almost imperceptible but enough to drive the great cat up toward the shelf on the wall. He hit the shelf with his forefeet and before his hind legs could catch up, neither the cat nor the shelf was there.

Panther failed to right himself. He landed on his flank, with the shelf still between his forepaws. He was winded for a moment but not hurt, and he shook his head several times before bending his nose to the piece of lumber he now gripped. Sniffing deeply, he closed his eyes and let the scent roll inward and drug him. The euphoria that flowed over him masked out all reality and the scent was all there was.

When the shelf had torn loose from the wall, a quarter-inch nylon line had slipped off a three-inch common nail on the top of the plank, over which it had been looped. Lashing like a thin white snake, the line had whipped out through a hole in the roof and across the downward slope, dislodging several shingles and two irate herring gulls on the way. The rope seemed to have a life of its own and to be hell-bent on its own destiny. The weighted sliding door that had begun to slide downward as soon as the nylon noose slipped free of its anchor point hit bottom with a thud and effectively sealed the larger of the cabin's two rooms from the outside world. But Panther didn't know that. He was still sensuously involved with his displaced shelf. For the moment, at least, he was operating in a different space-time continuum.

The idea that cats never fall because of their own miscalculations or that they are never hurt in a fall is an old wives' tale. Cats do fall and although they are amazingly supple and breathtakingly agile, they can be hurt. It was no great surprise to Panther that the shelf had collapsed or that he had landed on the cabin's floor with an undignified thud. He had fallen before, he had misjudged, miscalculated and just plain missed.

The door made a very distinct sound as it hit, but Panther was preoccupied at the moment and didn't take any particular notice of it. Although he got up and moved around the smaller room once or twice, he spent almost the entire hour following his mishap romantically involved with the piece of scrap lumber. He mewed and purred and sniffed the wood and rubbed his cheeks against it with eyes half closed and ears laid back. It was as near to ecstasy as he could get. He was thoroughly engrossed for the full time and then small things began to slip into place and he stopped his purring, stopped his mewing, stopped caressing the wood. He stood up sharply and coughed softly once. Somehow he had been alerted.

Perhaps, even after an hour, he remembered the sound of the door falling into place. Perhaps he suddenly noticed the changed light value or perhaps he was able to detect that the flow of air within the cabin was not the same as he had known it to be on past mouse-hunting expeditions. Something was different, something had been altered, and by that altogether dumbfounding ability cats have of detecting the slightest change in familiar surroundings, Panther knew something was wrong. He coughed softly again and moved toward the door that separated the two rooms. His ears were half back and his lips lifted slightly in the corners. Panther was not only trapped, he knew he was. And like some of his kind, but only some, he was not resigned. He was ready to fight.

It was just past seven o'clock in the evening when Panther first realized his predicament. It was not until two hours later that he gave up trying to claw the door apart. Then he sat back to examine what his incredible exertions had wrought. For those two hours he had dug his claws into the wood and tugged, and had literally drummed his paws against the wood between raking movements. He had snarled and come close to shrieking in rage. No one can say if Panther fully understood his plight or what the measure of his fear might have been, but his anger was plain to see and hear. It could, in fact, be heard over a quarter of a mile away, where an old man sat hunched over in his small rowboat, nibbling toothlessly on half a sandwich. Doc Painter lifted his rheumy eyes and listened, contemplating the sound of the first panther he had ever owned. He decided he liked the sound and decided to wait until noon of the following day before offering the cat any water. By that time, the old man figured, he would have "screamed hisself dry." He would appreciate both the water and the old man better by then. Now that the old man had his cat, he had to break him, to force him to submerge his cat personality by any and all means possible, for that was the most important part of the exercise. The old man, who was known to all around as the greatest panther tracker the Glades had ever seen, would now walk in those places where he was known with a great male panther at his heels. It was the final indignity he would visit on the species of cat that had given him a reason for living. It would be the outcome of his last hunt. Such were his dreams that day.

Freedom of movement, freedom of choice, is the essence of being wild. A cat, any wild creature, exists as a reality only when it is free to follow every instinct, every whim, every stimulating combination of both that may come his way. A bird in a cage, however large and well kept, is not a bird in the sky. A pinioned swan in a pond that is little more than a manicured and siphoned bowl is not the same as a whistler or trumpeter overhead, and a cat in a cabin, trapped by wit and planks of wood, is not wholly a cat. It was an ironic and perhaps sad commentary that the old man who had lived in the wild and known the wildcats that had come before Panther should not have known this. He less than almost anyone else could be forgiven for his ignorance. He had come about as close to living like an animal himself as a man can come, and his morality was as much a cat's as man's.

Like a fish that is pulled from the sea and begins losing its irridescence in seconds, Panther was a less luminous cat as he sat back on his haunches, rolled his head over to the side and spit halfheartedly at the door his claws had failed to devastate. He was no longer a wild thing but a thing driven wild by the foolish display of wit that had become so important to the old man. In the wild, Panther had served purposes far too profound for the old man to comprehend. As a prisoner in the cabin, he served none at all worth acknowledging.

When the old man appeared outside of the cabin exactly at noon the following day, Panther was crouched in a far corner of the smaller room. A dozen times he had tried the windows, tried to fit out between the solidly anchored two-by-fours and failed. He had tried the floor and found that he couldn't tear the boards free, although his claws dug satisfactorily into the aged and moisture-softened wood. He had tried the door again and had collapsed a three-legged table when he leaped upon it to try to claw down the ceiling. Without the table to help him he had leaped at the ceiling ten times, twenty times, a hundred times, in an effort to rip it apart and climb out and upward, to climb free of the room and its stench, free into the clear and relatively cool air that now lay so tantalizingly beyond. A dozen times he had hung from the rafters by his claws, had swung there briefly before dropping and spitting upwards, outwards at nothing in particular but at everything in general. He was frantic, furious and frightened. He was also thirsty.

Now, panting, with his ears laid back, the panther crouched in a corner of the small room and waited for the world to come to him with its next challenge, its new opportunities. He spit with unconcealed hatred as the old man's face appeared at the window between the slats of wood that made the cabin a prison. The old man peered in with no effort to hide his excitement. He whistled and whewed admiringly. He called out to the cat and cackled as his prisoner spit and snarled himself into a deeper fury. The old man was not ready for what followed, for he had killed so many cats so easily that he could not think of them as a menace. But for that instant at least, Panther was.

Before the man could react, Panther was across the small room, hurling his full weight against the two-by-fours. The paw with claws extended came out between the prison bars faster than Doc Painter had realized any creature could move. It really didn't seem like a continuous movement. It seemed more like disjointed events. A cat in the corner and a cat at the window — with nothing in between!

The slashing claws barely missed the old man's face as he went over backwards. He didn't have time for so much as a single curse. He fell over eighteen inches off the up-ended box and was lucky to survive with all of his brittle bones intact. On the ground he *did* curse; he cursed and vowed to have his vengeance.

Slower now, because he ached and because he was not just a little bit frightened, the old man righted the box, picked up his rifle from where it leaned against the shack and climbed up to peer in again at the window. He leaned the barrel of his rifle on the sill to brace himself and screamed in at the cat, "*I could'a killed ya easy any time I wanted to. I could'a nailed yer hide whenever I wanted it. Don't act like that t'me, goddamn ya! I still can.*"

Panther lashed out again, passing close enough to the man to set him teetering a second time on his insecure perch. But this time he had the gun to brace himself with and he didn't fall. He was no less furious, though, and fired blindly into the room. The bullet tore past Panther's head a foot high and punched a ragged hole in the wall beyond. The noise, though, didn't miss its mark and sent Panther flying away into the larger room, where he crouched low and hummed to himself. His ears were ringing from the monstrous boxing the sound of the exploding cartridge had given them. He was stunned and partially deafened. The old man stood outside and listened, wondering whether he had slain his cat in his anger, had in his haste shot a fish in a barrel.

He walked around the cabin and peered in through a peep-hole his sloppy carpentry of the previous week had provided and saw his cat crouching down in a far corner, shaking his head from time to time as if to rid himself of a troublesome mite. His trouble was not so easily disposed of, however. The explosion that had occurred inches from his ear had developed over three thousand foot-pounds of energy before the cat was even aware that an explosion had occurred. He had been slammed in his sensitive ears by a shock wave of staggering proportions. His nasal passages had been burned by the stink of the burning gases. His eyes had been temporarily affected as well.

The old man stared at the sickened cat, not at all sure of his own reactions or of what he wanted to do next. He had been subjected to several indignities, one of them being fear and another uncontrolled rage. He had suffered these at the dispo-sition of the cat whose life he had, in his own eyes, saved by not killing it. He saw himself as the cat's benefactor. He saw himself as a kind soul who could have killed and had not, and who had been endangered, in a sense injured, and certainly insulted for his pains, for his efforts at humanity. To this man, this strange man full of years, each one of which had known death, no cat had the right to live, except by his leave. Cats were for killing and he, in having spared this one, performed an unaccountably large act of charity. How then, why then, should the cat act in this way?

Panther was not long in picking the old man up at the peephole. He saw the eye staring in and stared back, snarling softly. The old man with his killer instincts stared at the cat. The old man, not the cat, felt embarrassment. He didn't know what to say. He had addressed more words in the past half century to the carcasses of cats he had slain than to men he had known. He had to say something, now that he had a cat alive.

"I'll be back, goddamn ya. I'll be back. Maybe timaarah ya'll want some water. It's gonna git hot in that cabin. Maybe timaarah ya'll be thirsty enough to come around. Actin' thata way to me . . ."

🌿 12 🌿

THROUGHOUT THE NIGHT THE TEMPERATURE IN THE CABIN remained above eighty. By seven o'clock the next morning it had begun climbing again. By ten it was ninety-two; by noon it was a hundred and two. Panther had been without food for three days, but much more important, he had been without water for almost sixty hours. By three o'clock the old man still had not come and the temperature within the airless shack passed one hundred and ten.

While Panther paced back and forth between the two

rooms, feeling his strength ebbing, the old man sat in his boat six miles away. It was tied to a crumbling dock that was connected by an elevated boardwalk to his incredibly ramshackle cabin. He sat in his boat, staring off toward Bitterroot, brooding. His feelings were hurt, and his pride, and he didn't know what to do. He did know that he didn't want the panther now that he had him. A vestigial sense of honor, or pride, or self-imposed rule of some sort, would keep him from shooting the trapped animal. Another, less complicated element in his makeup would also keep him from giving him back his freedom. Once he had fixed his sights on a cat, however those sights might be mounted, the cat could never again wander its range. Doc Painter was a panther hunter, the greatest, he was sure, who had ever stalked the Glades, and the obligations this honor carried with it, although unknown to any other human being and vague to the old man himself, were profound. They had to be. In the name of sanity and sense of self, they had to be.

The old man let the day slip away without returning to Bitterroot and Panther spent another airless, waterless night. By dawn of the next day, the beginning of his fourth in captivity, he was barely able to move from one room to the other. He slapped ineffectually at a board here, sniffed a plank there. Once or twice he managed to rise up onto his hind legs and rake the door, but he would soon thump down again with a groan, waver for a minute as he stood, and sink back onto his flank. Time was running out. By eleven o'clock in the morning he had passed out, literally fainted, and that was the way the old man found him when he peered in through a chink in the wall for the first time in forty-eight hours.

Doc Painter was genuinely remorseful, for he was certain the cat was dead. But then he saw the shallow rise and fall of the rib cage and ran down to his boat, where he retrieved the can he had brought along. He filled it with water and brought it to the sliding door he had fashioned with such care. Using a two-by-four as a pry and a section of log as a stop, he got the door up about a foot and a half and pushed the can inside. It jiggled as it was pushed across the rough floor by a pole, and the water slopped over its sides. The smell of it reached deep down into the oblivion through which Panther was easing and called him back. He twitched, he sniffed, although his eyes were still closed, and slowly he came to. He sat up slowly and then drank, drank until a gallon was gone — a full gallon of water. Bloated, distended, Panther sank back on his side and watched the old man peering in under the door. He didn't charge; he didn't even spit. He just stared back and ignored the raccoon carcass that was sent across the floor to him. Later that night he scraped together as much debris as he could find in the cabin and tried to bury the untouched coon.

Doc Painter had fastened a line to the water can and withdrew it the next morning, refilling it and slipping it back in again under the door. He offered Panther the carcasses of a couple of hybrid ducks and let the door slam back down into place. The foot and a half which he had raised the door had been enough to give Panther an opportunity to escape. At least it could have been tempting, but for some reason the trapped cat didn't try. With quiet resignation he sat across the room from the door, watching with keen interest the moves the man made as he retrieved his can, supplied fresh water and shoved the duck carcasses inside. He watched and waited, as if he knew that there would be other stages to come in this strange new relationship.

After the old man let the door slip down for the second time, he sat back against it on the outside and tried to sort things out in his mind. Except when it came to tracking wildcats, he had never been very analytical. He tossed aside, brushed away, anything that looked like it might bother him and had, in fact, come very close to being totally inarticulate in his later years. Since conversation with other men usually entailed questions to be answered or things to be considered, he very seldom bothered to engage himself in conversation of any kind. In the store run by Indians over along the Trail, he could get by with pointing and occasionally grunting and that is why he usually went there for the few necessities he could not supply himself.

But now he had to think, even to reach a decision. He had to figure out whether he liked caring for the trapped cat. If he decided that he didn't, he would have to come to some kind of decision as to what he wanted to do about it. His earlier fantasies about walking through town with the cat tagging after him had faded away. That would have eventually, inevitably, led to questions, conversation, prying eyes, all the things he had spent his life avoiding. It was to be, this vision of a man and his panther, the last shred of gregariousness he would ever fantasize. Like so many other things in the old man's long and lonely life, it would never materialize. It could no more come to be than the dreams he had had as he lay awake on his bare cot sixty years before and twitched and turned and sweated his way through one fantastic love affair after another. He had felt his own heartbeat as a throbbing in his temple and he had called out loud, screamed into the night. He had clawed his way through his fantasies one by one until exhaustion overtook him. He had been a lonely boy then, with lonely dreams that came again and again to haunt him. This one last dream, perhaps in its own way as sexual as the others, was never any closer to reality than its predecessors sixty years before had been.

As the old man sat with his back against the sliding door, he could hear Panther move up to the other side of the panel and sniff. He could hear the cat move his nose along the cracks and inhale deeply, snuffling up the scent of the man, trying to understand him by his stench alone.

The old man pressed his head back against the door and listened. He was strangely pleased that the cat was trying to know him. It was as if the cat were trying to find something redeeming in him, something so good that he would forgive him for the numbers of his kind he had slain and for trapping him into his own feline ignominy. The old man listened, his facial expression arrested, his senses transfixed, as the cat snuffled and sniffed only inches from his head. He didn't want to move, he didn't want to breathe, he never wanted the strange tingling sensation to stop. The dryness in his mouth, the itchy feeling in his throat, all were part of a strange syndrome, a strange sensuousness of which the cat has almost always been a symbol. But he couldn't hold it any longer. Fingers were creeping across the roof of his mouth as his head lolled back, his rheumy eyes unseeing; itchy fingers had found his throat and he coughed, struggle as he would against it.

Inside Panther bolted, tipping his water can over as he burst in headlong flight toward the small room in the back. Doc Painter cursed, but he didn't move.

The old man sat until nearly midnight, waiting, hoping the cat would come back and join him in secret communion. But the cough had been ill-timed; it had been an infraction of the rule of silence that is essential to those few, rare transcendant moments a man may know in his lifetime. With the panther inches from his ear, a wildcat trying to translate the stink of an unwashed old man, that old man had come as close as he ever had to a religious experience, or to a sexual one. He would never come that close to either again. The pendulum of his life followed the same small arc it always had, but somehow the movements were not as crisp now, not as sure on the return swing.

The old man left just minutes before midnight. He went down to his boat and back to his shack on another island. He knew he would be back the following afternoon to feed and water his cat again, for in the dark hours he had been able to think through a course of action. Somehow, in some strange way, he had even been able to recognize the irony in his own plan. He had chuckled out loud and heard the cat stir in the shack. The cat was more finely tuned now than he had ever been before and the old man understood that well enough. In a matter of days the cat would make an effort to escape, he was sure. It would come as the old man fed and watered him. The old man would foil him, though; he would be able to foil him because he knew the effort would come. Doc Painter was glad that it would come, because it justified his plan, the long-range plan that had given him his brief moment of mirth. In the meantime, Doc Painter knew, the cat was watching, timing him. It was an exquisite war and the old man was prepared to love it.

The plan was simple, direct and based on realities, the realities of the old man's needs. To release the cat was unthinkable. The thought of it being free to wander, free to hunt, negated the old man's entire life. In freeing his cat he would be freeing all the others, all those he had slain. Without them permanently dead his life had no meaning whatsoever. Even he knew that that was all there was.

The alternatives to releasing the panther, that unthinkable act, were few. He could shoot it through a crack in the wall and solve the whole matter in a single violent moment that was like so many others he had known. It was, after all, not very different, shooting a cat in a shack and shooting one off the branch of a tree. It was the same kind of death, the same kind of moment in the lives of cat and hunter alike. Yet that wasn't the answer either. That was too anticlimactic, too *something else* the man couldn't verbalize to himself. But where he did not have the words he had the feelings, and he ruled out that alternative as impossible.

No, the man would care for his cat. He would bring him food and water every day and perhaps the cat would even come to the door again and carry the man off by way of his senses to places within himself where he had never been before. But of course the old man was realistic. He was eighty and he might be coming upon his own death in the immediate future. What then? What would become of his cat? The old man had found the ironic answer only after hours in the dark, hours of knowing that the well-spooked cat was sitting across a room, staring balefully with great yellow eyes at the door against which he leaned. The old man in the midst of his tingling communion with the unseen cat decided that as soon as he felt death coming on, he would bring the cat a great feast and many cans of water. He would shove them under the door and go away to die. He would tell no one of his cat; he would make no other provisions. His cat would die after him. His cat would be a sacrifice. But, he reasoned, he might die suddenly, he might sicken without warning and be unable to return to Bitterroot. *No matter,* he thought, *the cat will still die after me wondering when I'm coming back, wanting me to, missing me. Maybe then he'll wish he could hear me sneeze,* the foolish old man thought petulantly. *Maybe then.*

⚘ 13 ⚘

THE LARGER OF THE CABIN'S TWO ROOMS NOW CONTAINED the uneaten carcasses of one raccoon, two ducks, several fish and a mongrel dog, the victim of a speeding car that the old man had found next to the Trail one morning. The stench was almost unbearable as the old man squatted down at the bottom of the door and began reaching for them with a rake he had attached to a long pole.

"What do ya eat, damn ya?"

It had been a week now and although Panther was drinking

some of the water that was brought to him every day, he was still refusing to eat. He was losing weight and Doc Painter could see enough of him in the dark corners where he lurked to notice the change. The one contingency the old man hadn't figured on was the cat dying before him. He had no intention of exhausting himself by thinking that whole thing through again. It had to go the way he had planned.

The next day, Panther's eighth as a prisoner, a live chicken was thrust under the door. It ran clucking foolishly across the room. By reflex a tawny paw pinned it, crushed it and held it firm as the last useless struggling ebbed into stillness. When the chicken died Panther withdrew his paw. He licked it and it tasted pleasantly of chicken. He sniffed the bird and tentatively pulled loose a mouthful of feathers. He pulled a few more loose and then drew the chicken closer. The old man peered in under the door and held his breath. Then Panther ate and the old man felt tears at the corners of his eyes. He had no idea at all why they were there.

Each day the old man brought Panther live food. He soon ran out of chickens and the clucking that had always gone on under his cabin was a thing of the past. He managed to take an occasional duck by liming a log on which he placed a handful of cracked corn and he trapped an opossum one day and a raccoon on another. He kept live fish in a barrel near his cabin door and carried them to Bitterroot in old gallon oilcans. He was intent on keeping Panther alive, for no other reason than that that was the plan.

Panther took the live food every day and his weight loss eventually reversed itself. Each day he crouched back in a corner as he heard the old man struggling up the slight slope from the beach. He crouched and he waited as the door inched up and the water bucket was withdrawn on the end of its line. He watched as the new bucketful was pushed in ahead of a pole and as the mouth of the burlap sack was shoved toward him. Always the old man lay flat on the old porch and stared in under the door. Satisfied that the cat was off across the room, he would reach in and untie the sack. Slowly the sack would be withdrawn and then tipped up at the last minute as Panther's living prey was dumped out. He would usually kill almost immediately in a single easy spring. There was never much of a struggle, rarely even any noise.

At any time Panther could have finished the old man and made good his escape. There was no place in the cabin, certainly no place in the larger room, from which he could not have reached the door in a fraction of the time it would have taken Doc Painter to withdraw his arms. A single leap would have taken him there. It is doubtful that Doc Painter would have been able to withstand the shock to his system that would have followed the damage Panther's claws and teeth could have done to his arms. The door was always raised just enough so that Panther could have wriggled free. But Panther had accepted his fate and the try for freedom Doc Painter had predicted never came. The old man came to recognize in time that he had been wrong and began placing his arms in jeopardy only after being reasonably certain of that fact.

Had the old man been able to concentrate on the whole problem a second time, he would have recognized that Panther was in fact becoming the instrument of his death rather than the other way around. Through his appetite for both food and water and through the old man's resolve to keep the cat alive, a form of tyranny had come to exist. Doc Painter was far too old and in too poor a condition to do the amount of work he was finding forced upon him. Every day he poled the twelve-mile round trip; every day he carried a gallon of water up the steep embankment and every day he had to capture live food to carry to his cat. Panther's weight loss had been reversed, but the old man's was progressing well.

On the third morning of the third week of Panther's imprisonment, the old man awoke to a new sensation. He was seriously ill and he knew it. His left leg ached unbearably and his left side, just below his rib cage, felt as if the area were in flames. He stared at the ceiling and tried to focus his eyes on its details. It was several minutes before he could pick out the odds and ends of his hermit's life that hung there. The extra anchor came into focus first, then the floats he had once found off the end of his dock following a storm. The bent propeller to the outboard motor he had never quite managed to own finally took on a firm outline and then the several old medicine bottles that hung by strings around their necks. He had picked both the propeller and the bottles off a junk heap but had never found a use for any of them. Slowly the whole ceiling came into perspective and he tried to sit up. It was a painful effort and a slow one, but he finally managed to slip his legs off the bed and let his feet find the floor. He sat there for several minutes, wondering what was wrong, and then he knew. He was dying, he decided, finally dying after all this time. He tried to determine if he was frightened and came to the conclusion that he was not. But he was worried because he had a lot to do before the end came. A man, after all, is obligated to put his estate in order.

Sometime back he had made up his mind to shoot a deer for his cat's last meal. He was sure the panther would accept a dead deer even if he did insist that his other food be served alive. The old man had to hunt down and kill a deer and get it over to his cat before he died. It was a lot to worry about.

It had been some months since the old man had hunted anything larger than a raccoon or a duck and although he had cartridges for his .22 and shells for his single-shot 20-gauge, he had none for his old lever-action Winchester .32 Special.

It took Doc Painter nearly an hour to get himself into his overalls and to pull his shoes on over his filthy, bare feet. He knelt in front of his homemade stove and shoved a woodbox aside with a great deal of effort. Using a broken knife blade, he pried a board up and rummaged around in the cavity until he found the tin cup. He slowly counted out his life savings — it came to sixty-four cents. *Enough for four rounds,* he reasoned, and that was all he would need to see his final ambition on earth accomplished.

It took the panther hunter several hours to pole his small flat-bottomed boat south to the Trail and he fell into the muddy water as he tried to beach it. He lost a shoe in the bottom muck and in disgust threw his other one into the boat and started out on the four-mile trek to the store barefooted. He stared straight ahead as he walked, his eyes fixed on eternity. Mercifully, he didn't feel the pain as his feet blistered and swelled. He was oblivious to the midday heat that beat down on him, baked what was left of him and bounced off the road ahead almost to blind him. Cars flew past at sixty miles an hour and more. They whistled by, hammering his frail body with their hot winds and fumes, but he didn't notice them. The only burden he felt was the burden of his plan, the burden of Panther's last meal. He stumbled forward like a dead man who had somehow retained the power of movement.

No one noticed the old man come in through the screen door; at least no one later claimed to have noticed. When Buck Henry walked over to where the old man stood, he was startled and then frightened by what he saw. Doc Painter stood in front of the counter in the small, dingy store with both hands clenched into fists. His knuckles were pressed down on the counter top and he stared straight ahead. He was shivering, his whole frame vibrating as he stood in two pools of blood. His feet were cut in at least a dozen places and the substance of his life, substance he could no longer afford to spare, marked his tracks across the floor and accumulated at an alarming rate where he stood. He was drooling and his bottom lip sagged grotesquely. He had become incontinent during his trek and his overalls were stained in a pitifully revealing way. Buck Henry stared into the old man's face and asked in a timid voice, *"Doc? Sumpin' wrong, Doc?"*

The young intern exhaled violently against the stench in the ambulance. He thought several things to himself in which he could take no pride and bent again over the old man as the Cadillac with flashing red lights and wailing siren streaked back down the Tamiami Trail. His stethoscope had confirmed his suspicions and the young doctor pressed the oxygen mask against Doc Painter's face in a first step to counteract the old man's pneumonia. *Malnutrition,* the young man from Chicago mused, *and God alone knows what else.* In his mind the intern gave Doc Painter twenty-four hours to live, if he was lucky.

Coming from Chicago, of course, the new doctor had never known a panther hunter from the Glades before.

Panther had no conscious awareness of time as such, but like all wild things, he could detect an interruption in a life rhythm. He had set his inner clock by the old man's habits. The hunter had always fed and watered him by two o'clock in the afternoon. When he failed to appear by seven and the night birds began to call, Panther paced his prison impatiently. The offerings the hunter had brought him each day were small and although enough to sustain him, he was hungry every day, ready and anxious to eat. What the old man in his dotage had never come to realize was that once Panther had broken the ice by killing and eating that first chicken he would have accepted dead food as well as live. It was his initial reaction to captivity that kept him from eating, not aversion to dead food. The hunter could have fed his cat less often and in larger quantities. There was still water left in his can from the day before — he was drinking much less than the gallon the old man always provided — but there was no food. Panther paced and whistled softly and then grunted. He was displeased. Since the man had become his prisoner he liked things to be done according to schedule.

The attending physician finished his examination and made several notations on a clipboard form. While one ward attendant rolled oxygen cylinders into place by the head of the bed, another helped the nurse wash the old man's body before rolling him over onto the clean sheet that was being unfolded on top of a rubber pad.

The doctor finished his report and turned to the geriatric ward nurse. He spoke in a flat, professionally muted voice: "If he should regain consciousness, try to find out his name and anything you can about his family. Might as well get in touch with them now. He won't last."

The plastic tent was put in position over the top half of Doc Painter's bed. The lights in the ward were turned down and the old man, bathed and on clean sheets for the first time in his adult life, breathed on. His dreams were his secret and his secret was locked away in his dreams.

The shadows had flowed across Bitterroot and entered the water in the slough to the west. The day animals were away in their places and the night creatures were already abroad. The killing had started and the sounds of execution were everywhere. Panther grunted as he made his hundredth circuit of the two rooms within the space of an hour. His feet plomped down in front of each other in careless grace. His shoulders rippled and his pendulous stomach swung loosely from side to side. He reached up with his nose and sniffed but couldn't pick up a trace of the old man. He grunted again and continued his forward movement to nowhere. And way, way beyond the coast of Florida, the weather began to develop into a strange new pattern. It was September, hot September, and as Doc Painter faced his death in unaccustomed cleanliness and Panther his fate in his now familiar prison, Dora, the fourth tropical storm of the season, gathered her strength and sharpened her resolve.

❧ 14 ❧

THE FIRST SIGN OF RADICALLY DROPPING PRESSURE WITHIN
the huge tropical air mass had occurred over water, far from
land. It had been nearly seventy-two hours before it was detected and reported. The radio message from the Algerian
freighter had been somewhat vague as to position, but it was
clear enough in substance. It reported to the National Hurri-
can Center in Miami that a tropical storm far to the south and
east of Florida was shaping up and would bear watching. It

was the kind of report that sets complicated technical wheels in motion.

Torrential rains moved ahead of the swirling mass and it became clear after four days that its erratic course had leveled out and that Puerto Rico was in its path. After two days of frantic activity Puerto Rico was ready. The storm hit and three people died, according to news reports. Actually the number was eleven, but eight of them were nameless squatters, not the sort of people of whom either news or statistics are made.

The West Indies were next and the smashing force of the winds apparently increased. Anguilla was first, with four dead; Antigua was next, with five. Barbuda was hardest hit of all and thirteen known people lost their lives. A private plane out of Georgetown with four people aboard became the next casualty and the toll mounted. For almost a week Dora flipped back and forth, south and generally east of the Florida peninsula. Although it was clear that the storm was far too violent just to peter out, it still wasn't clear whether it would move north or head west across the Caribbean. There had been too many deaths already for anyone to expect sudden benevolence. This was a killer storm. Of course, it was possible that it could pass toward the north and east of the mainland. It was just that no one really expected it to.

Then, quite suddenly, the course was set. The storm began moving north, then northwest, then west. Its eye passed straight down "hurricane alley" — the ninety-mile-wide strip of sea between Florida's southern tip and Cuba — reversed itself, moved eastward, corrected to a northward track, struck between Marathon and Tavernier Key and whipped across the coast toward the heart of Florida.

The men who worry about storms were on top of Dora all the way. They knew her eye to be twenty miles across, her calm, low-pressure eye. Specially reinforced Super-G Constellations flew into it and circled there to keep track of the vicious lady's peregrinations. The men knew, too, that the storm reached up over thirty thousand feet and that the radius outward from the eye was over two hundred miles. The winds varied in strength but generally sustained their velocity at a hundred and fifteen miles an hour. Gusts, of course, reached much higher; up to a hundred and thirty miles had been recorded before the Weather Bureau mast was torn away and lost.

There were no weather fronts as such involved, for the storm had been born in a single tropical air mass. Since the eye was a low-pressure area, the direction of the winds had reversed at birth and were running counterclockwise as the storm moved toward the North American mainland.

Panther knew the storm was coming. All the animals of the Everglades did, at least all of those who lived a life exposed to air. And no one can say for certain that even those within the envelope of the Everglades water didn't know it as well, for the approach of the storm was attended by many changes, only a small portion of which were subtle. Here was something even a man could sense, which means that its symptoms were gross indeed.

As the storm moved closer, the barometric pressure dropped. This alone, in all probability, told most animals above the surface of the water that they were in probable jeopardy. There was a terrible stillness in the air and an ashy-gray quality to the sky, although no clouds were yet in view. Somehow clear blue had turned to gray and the ability of the water to mirror the world above changed, dulled, faded and then all but vanished.

The second clue to the changes that were about to occur was the sudden appearance of birds from the shore, a few at first, plainting their irritation, then scores, then hundreds, then a symphony of tens of thousands. Even the smallest hammocks that had harbored hundreds of birds now bore the weight of thousands as the flow inland increased. In places it seemed as if every branch, every reed, every solid object in view, bore its share of the winged burden. Telephone wires along Route 41 were lined as far as the eye could see and a dozen species joined the usual contingent of kingfishers in soldierly rows.

Windless, gray, with the pressure slipping downward, populated with new birds in uncounted numbers, the Everglades waited. It was the time of hush before the time of hell.

Even on a calm day there is *some* movement of air across the broad saw-grass flats. The sea is too close on all sides, the open land and inland waters too exposed to the Atlantic and the Gulf, for the air to be ever really still for long. But now the air was still. The incredible swirling air mass that was the hurricane seemed to be pushing a mourning silence on ahead of it, to prepare those about to die. Not a blade of grass moved, not a leaf trembled on its stem, and each bird sat rigidly still on its perch or moved only reluctantly when another came to rest nearby and unsettled those already there. The depth of the gray became more profound with every minute that passed. The temperature stood at one hundred and one degrees and the humidity lay across the world like a suffocating blanket of near-mist.

With the eye of the storm still two hundred and fifty miles away, Panther paced within his prison, more terrified now by the enclosure that held him than at any time since his capture. He tried the door again and then he stood on his hind legs for the thousandth time and tried to push his way through the improvised bars that blocked the window, the rough two-by-fours nailed in place by Doc Painter. When neither the door nor the windows would give, he retested the boards on the floor and threw himself upward against the ceiling. He hung there briefly, his claws hooked into the beams, and then dropped again to all fours. Looking up, he spat explosively in his frustration and then continued his pacing. He moved clockwise, consistently and often brushed against the wall and the doorjamb as he passed from room to room. There were half a dozen places where his coat was rubbed bare along his left side. As the pressure dropped and the stillness that was a prelude to the ultimate explosion deepened, Panther's pace quickened. He was trapped at a time when only complete freedom could give him the barest chance of survival. Strangely, in his own way, he seemed to know it. His nervousness was so pronounced that it seemed as if he really did understand his plight.

The nurse checked each bed every hour. Unless there were other orders to interrupt her routine or unless a frantically pulled cord flashed a light over her desk and sent her hurrying down the hall, that was the attention the old and the dying received. There wasn't a patient in the ward for whom a place could be found in the intensive-care units; there were none for whom surgery was planned. The ward the silently moving nurse supervised was an exclusive club. It was for those for whom all had been done except the administration of a last-minute bit of comfort and, where possible, a last-minute portion of dignity. Since there is precious little dignity in death, in its immediacy or in the fear of it, there wasn't too much the nurse could do but try. Her professional life was a morbid treadmill. Each death blended in with all the others. The distinctions were harder to find, the demarcations less important with every day that passed.

The old man barely regained consciousness for a brief five minutes in the nurse's presence and she never had managed to get his name or any information about his non-existent family. Twice she had gone by his bed and stopped to listen while he whispered frantically about "th' cat," but she wasn't able to make anything of what he was saying, and moved on to other, more immediate duties. Delirium was all around her, every day, and she missed the significance of a hundred frantic messages entrusted to her for every one she got. A bedpan, a cry for water, or a patient violently protesting the steel rails beside the bed — these are far more immediate projects in a darkened room than the disjointed words that tumble forth on the shallow breath of a dying man.

Because it had been over an hour since she had seen him and because she fully expected to find him dead each time she stopped to check him, the nurse was doubly startled to find Doc Painter's bed empty. At first she stopped to think, to sort things out, for she wasn't at all sure whether the old man had already died and been removed. But no! She remembered it had been another old man several beds down the line. The old man with pneumonia, the old man whose card said *John*

Doe/"Doc" Age: Unk/Est 80, the old man who was supposed to die, had come to within the space of the preceding sixty-five minutes and walked — or crawled — out of the ward.

Moving rapidly, the nurse checked all the obvious places. When she couldn't find him in the linen closet, in the ladies' or the gentlemen's toilet or on the stair landings, she called the front desk and reported the disappearance. Although the man's whereabouts was obviously a matter of life and death, it was fully a quarter of an hour before a search of the building and the grounds got under way. The life and the death of *John Doe/"Doc"* were no longer of great concern to society. Only last-minute comfort and his last-ditch dignity were really at stake, for the rest was considered fore-ordained.

The spinning air mass, still four hundred miles across, sent small fingers of high-velocity air out in jets as it whirled at nearly one hundred and twenty miles an hour, shifting and shuttling toward the northwest at fifteen miles an hour. The small jets shot across the coastline a good twenty miles ahead of the storm mass itself. The sea beneath the fingers was piled up, moving toward land in a kind of low wall, for the storm tide had formed. As the land underneath the tide edged up toward the beach, the mass of water built above it in a perverse counterratio. The blue that had turned to gray now turned to black. It was four o'clock in the afternoon and night had fallen, the storm night, the wind night, the night of death and destruction.

At the hospital the hunt for *John Doe/"Doc"* was called off. There were too many other things to be done, too many windows to shutter, too many patients to be moved away from windows. Beds were being wheeled into interior corridors, people were calling out instructions, and calling out in pain. The storm was minutes away and *John Doe/"Doc"* was forgotten. One way or another, it had been decided, he would turn up. In any case, it would all be the same in the end.

The first air projectiles from the storm reached Bitterroot and stung into the trees with an audible pop. They had hissed violently as they shot across the water, leaving a trail of disturbance and microscopic destruction. Mirror-smooth water trying unsuccessfully to reflect back a gray world to a gray sky was suddenly marked by thin slices of wind. Their paths were arrow-straight, for they had been spun off the main air mass at high velocities. They shot across still waters and cut through hammocks like blades of air. Then came the noise, in the distance at first and then building, decibel by decibel, until it was a savage sound that filled the whole world.

The first few drops of water fell almost as soon as the first jets reached the hammock. It was a matter of seconds between those first drops and the torrent. It was blinding, staggering in its fury, and leaves and birds alike were stripped from trees and dashed to the earth and water below.

At the first sound of the wind, followed as it was almost immediately by the first sound of the torrent, Panther went nearly mad. He threw himself against the walls, against the door, against the window. He bled in several places where protruding nails had torn his hide and he was fairly screaming with rage and terror.

Glass windows along the oceanfront to the east that had been improperly prepared exploded outward as the whirling air dropped the pressure on their outer surfaces, turning the air momentarily trapped within the buildings into bombs. Merchandise from fashionable shops was strewn helter-skelter and bathing suits lodged ludicrously on cabbage palms while a royal palm further up Collins Avenue was draped in amber Canadian mink for a fleeting instant.

A policeman huddled in his car and repeated again and again through a loudspeaker that looters would be arrested. He kept on repeating this message, perhaps in the desperation of his fear, even though no one could stand on the street outside. In fact, no one was in sight. His message stopped when the horn was ripped from the roof of his car. Minutes later his car, with him still inside, began tumbling before the wind. He held his microphone in one hand and his drawn pistol in the other as his car tumbled over and off into the canal. He dropped both as he fought unsuccessfully to open the car door.

Glass flew everywhere and in less fashionable areas along the coast, overhead wires ripped loose. Communications were eroded, then finally brought to an end as aerials and broadcasting towers toppled and telephone lines disappeared under mountains of palm fronds. Then the sea in its piled-up storm tide moved onto the land and people could no longer recognize the streets on which they lived. Water cascaded everywhere and the smaller homes shuddered under the impact. A great many just gave up and collapsed and others were washed or blown away.

Doc Painter had had to stumble almost a quarter of a mile through the hospital parking lot and the undeveloped land beyond before he found a small dock with a dinghy tied to it.

The boat didn't belong to anyone in particular, since it had been left behind several years before by an intern heading north for his residency. It was for anyone's use who desired it and was in fact occasionally pressed into service for short fishing trips by hospital personnel.

The first wind fingers were just knifing across the parking lot as Doc Painter stumbled forward into the boat. He was completely disoriented, totally contained within himself, as with automatic motions he untied the short, worn bowline. He stood and took the pole and pushed off as the jets of wind slashed in beside him on parallel courses. He stood there, poling his boat, heaven alone knows into which dream, a very old man dressed in a hospital shift. His legs and his back were bare except for the four neat little bows the nurse had tied behind him to hold the gown in place.

The old man's voyage was a hundred yards old when the rain struck. His knees fairly buckled under the impact from above. He turned slowly and stared up into the sky, screwing his eyes shut against the rain. His white hair streamed in the wind. He moved his lips and mumbled. The driving rain was pulling his hospital shift down over his shoulders. The top came undone, then the second bow, and then there was a small pile of white at the man's feet, standing out in sharp contrast to the gray world.

The radio tower on the hospital roof, the establishment's last contact with the outside, collapsed as the wind hit and seconds later the dock from which the old man had departed disappeared beneath the rising water that was moving up the river from the sea. The wind stung across the water, sounding like a thousand snakes. It reached the man almost instantly and as he turned, alone, quite naked and quite mad, he explained to anyone who would listen that he was going to Bitterroot to free his cat. His death was merciful. He neither felt it nor feared it because it happened to his body, which had been several worlds apart from his mind for nearly twenty-four hours. As his body and the boat in which it rode vanished before the wind and the water, the old man's soul moved off into its own eternal orbit and Doc Painter, the man who had slain two hundred panthers and captured one, ceased to exist.

𝕏 15 𝕏

THE EYE OF THE STORM WAS DESTINED TO PASS DIRECTLY across Bitterroot Island from the southeast to the northwest. Winds in excess of a hundred miles an hour were to batter the hammock for nearly eight hours before the storm reached the west coast and spun out across the Gulf, heading for Louisiana and Texas with its promise of more death and destruction. Of the 1.7 tropical storms of dangerous intensity that have smashed into the Florida peninsula every year since the history of the area was first recorded, the one that headed directly for the hammock on which Panther was a prisoner was the third worst known. The barometric pressure dropped below 27.00 inches and held there for hours. At one point it edged down to 26.65, bringing it to within a hair's breadth of being the all-time recorded low for the western hemisphere.

Panther's terror mounted as the storm approached. When the actual winds themselves began hammering in across the flats, flinging debris up into great windrows and uprooting trees, the cat was driven into an almost insane fury. In a time of mortal danger, when his instincts were churning within him, nothing could have been more cruel than the severe restriction of movement. He crashed around within the cabin, repeatedly hurling himself against the walls, the windows and the door. Flying vegetation began piling up in the crude latticework of the windows, hung up on the improvised wooden bars, and wet branches with dead birds laced through them dangled within a paw's reach. But Panther wasn't after birds; he was after freedom.

The roof of the shack admitted water even in a light rain. As it was bombarded by the incredible torrents that poured from the sky before the storm and throughout its peak hours, the inside of the panther's prison was a sopping morass of filthy water. It poured in faster than it could drain out. At times Panther stood in pools that covered his paws. As the space beneath the cabin became saturated and the water began creeping across the entire hammock, the cabin stopped draining altogether and the water became hock-deep. This made the cat even more hysterical than he had been before. He bled from a dozen places as his repeated assaults on the nail-studded walls resulted in more and deeper lacerations and punctures.

He vocalized his misery by screaming against the wind, bellowing his full range of cat sounds. But the noise of the wind and the rain was so loud and the racket made by flying debris so awful that it is doubtful that an exploding cannon could have been heard, even if there had been someone to hear it.

As the wind reached its ultimate intensity, bizarre, seemingly impossible things began to happen. In Miami, to the east, a soda straw, an ordinary straw torn loose from a container in a fountain that was all but totally destroyed by the storm, whistled down the street like a projectile and imbedded itself in a palm tree to the depth of an inch and a half. A thirty-six-foot cabin cruiser traveled two miles inland on the insane tide and missed having a collision until it came to a one-story dwelling. It traveled completely through the building, emerging on the far side with a grand piano in its cockpit. There were two passengers on the boat before it hit the house, and three afterwards. No one was hurt.

After the storm, several dozen people would report having seen dogs and cats sailing by in the sky, and in fact they would not be exaggerating. Hundreds, thousands of domestic animals not recovered in time by families forced into shelters or ordered by law officers to evacuate lowland areas were lost in the few hours of hell. The number of wild animals lost cannot even begin to be estimated, but certainly it was in the millions. A twelve-foot alligator would later be found forty feet up in a tree. Somehow the tree survived the storm; the alligator didn't.

On Bitterroot hell was all there was. The entire island was flooded at least to some degree and fifty percent of all the trees over ten feet tall were lost in the first thirty minutes. Somehow, though, the ramshackle little cabin held. Then, from across the flats, one of the weirdest sights of the storm appeared. Several enormous royal palms that had been uprooted nearly ten miles away tumbled across the open space in a great curving arc, prisoners of an unbelievably powerful gust of wind. End over end they came, like mad acrobats in an insane circus. The giants somersaulted through the storm like living symbols of a world gone wild. Most of the tumbling palms missed the hammock, but one came directly ashore where the cabin stood and in a moment there was a pile of rubble where the small building had been.

Eventually Dora passed, leaving a shuddering world of devastation in her wake. Throughout almost an entire night she had screamed and wailed and tortured everything she could reach. Her destruction had been wanton, indiscriminate, without purpose or pattern. She had been a dealer in death, a killer, a living force gone berserk.

Dawn found the waters receding from Bitterroot. There had been times when the entire hammock had gone under, but the actual shape of the land had altered little. It did, however, look like an entirely different landscape. Very few tall trees were left and almost everything over thirty feet leaned precariously toward the west. The waters surrounding the island were littered with thousands of bird carcasses and the bodies of mammals, small and large, were everywhere. In places, five and six dead deer could be seen within an area of an acre or less. In the water, floating, beginning to rot from within and bloat, were birds and beasts, and on the land, wherever it was dry, thousands of fish. Along the shore of Bitterroot and every other hammock in Dora's path, great piles of trees and brush were stacked, packed so tightly that men could not have pulled them apart. Animal life, plant life and lifeless muck were piled and cemented together in monuments to Dora's strength. The number of dead animals that were laced throughout the windrows can hardly be imagined. Those that lived were usually the smallest and in the first still hours of dawn they began to creep out into the open, a mouse here, a frog there, a turtle and then a slender, glassy-eyed snake. They didn't hunt each other, not right away, for they were truly stunned.

It was only a matter of hours after the storm had passed before the rotten-egg stink of hydrogen sulfide could be detected. As the decay of newly dead plants and animals progressed, the intensity of swamp gas increased. In three days it was blinding in its strength. The sun beat down and what had been wet became dry, then brittle, then dangerous. Fires broke out as electric storms came and went, releasing far more voltage than water, and soon fires could be seen burning furiously in a dozen areas around Bitterroot. To swamp gas was added smoke, to devastation was added fire, to death was added death, and many of the creatures that had managed to survive the storm succumbed to this latest calamity.

It was into this world of death and evil odors that Panther had emerged at dawn. He had streaked like a bit of tawny lightning into a windrow after the tumbling royal palm had devastated his prison. As the walls had buckled out at the corners from the crushing weight on the roof and been gripped by the wind, Panther had sped through the first opening he saw and plunged panic-stricken into the first shelter he could find. In the ensuing hours his leg had been broken by another tree that added its weight to the pile and he had nearly drowned as water flowed deep where he lay before he could free himself. But he had survived where few large animals had. He was injured but alive, barely alive, and the same could be said for the land and most of what it contained.

The shattered right front leg would take time to heal and Panther hobbled, keeping it free of the ground as much as possible. Fortunately, he didn't have to hunt. Although panthers are not generally attracted by carrion, they will eat it when necessary. There was carrion enough to feed a thousand cats and he moved from deer to pig to bear to raccoon, nibbling a bit of the rotting flesh here, eating a little more there.

The torrential rains that had marked the storm had left the water level high, but in a matter of days it began to reestablish a more normal level. Then the world of the Everglades began to rebuild itself, to seek again an economy of life, a balance and a working system of interrelationships. An ecosystem, like a rubber band, has a memory. No matter how it is stretched, it will try to re-form itself again.

The first wildlife to return were the birds. Thousands had escaped to the north and some to the more risky south, and now they began filtering back to reestablish their roosting sites and their rookeries. It was not many weeks after the storm had passed when the first fall migrants from the north appeared and in the waters there were fish again. Insect life had survived without a dent, for a billion bugs here or there really does not matter.

One day a raccoon wandered ashore on Bitterroot, heaven alone knows from where, and a few deer appeared the next evening. There were frogs and there were reptiles, and soon, although it still smelled of death and decay, Bitterroot began to witness the reestablishment of its animal community. Plants and trees began sending up new shoots and leaves appeared on branches that had been stripped. Through it all, as his leg slowly knitted and his other wounds healed, Panther moved slowly, cautiously seeking again a new rhythm for a life that had been disrupted and all but destroyed, first by an old man's folly, then by the hurricane.

Six weeks after the storm, after six weeks of knitting and the careful husbanding of strength, Panther killed a deer. He felt an agony of pain roar upward into his shoulder as the frantically bucking doe tried to tug free, bringing unbearable pressure to his recently injured leg, but he held on and ended the animal's life by seeking the base of her skull with his stabbing teeth. He drank her blood first, then he opened the animal's paunch and ate the viscera. He scraped a few leaves together and observed the careless ritual of covering the cache. He returned to it the next day, and the next, and then, after eating off the deer for the fourth time, Panther left Bitterroot Island, left the hammock he had claimed as his own long ago and headed into a new life. Once his island had meant security, stability, a safe place to be, a safe place to return to. But Doc Painter and Dora had conspired to change all that and his hammock could never again be the same. Now that his leg was healed, although there would be pain for several months when he was careless in its use, he was free to go, free to wander until he found another place that was without memories of sick old men and savage storms. He was once again the essence of life, a wild thing free to follow his wild ways. It had been ordained, long ago when the cat was designed, that its life should be one of danger and death. That is the way the cat was

built and that is the way he was fitted into the world that was
there before him. Without a job to do, without a niche to fill,
the cat would have been surplus and would have been destroyed in a world where plans are not so casually made. A
wild thing in a wild place has a wild life to lead as well as a
job to do. Panther was such a wild thing and the Everglades
is still such a place in part. The job and the life still lay ahead
of him and Bitterroot of the evil memories, by his own wild
choice, was to be no part of either. Panther, it must be remembered, had still not reproduced himself in kind and therefore
had not fulfilled his original purpose in life.

🌿 16 🌿

THERE WAS NO SPECIAL REASON, AT LEAST NONE THAT A
human being could discern, why Panther chose to move
toward the northeast once he left Bitterroot, but that was the
direction he selected. It was shortly after dawn when he
stepped off into the shallow water and headed across the open
flats toward a smaller hammock several miles away. He moved
along at a steady pace as the hammock grew larger and larger
before him. There were closer ones off to his left and his right,

but he had selected his target and kept himself on course toward it.

When he was about a hundred and fifty yards short of the little hammock, a thudding roar split the world apart and an airboat came skidding around the north end of the island, ploughing up a ridge of water before it. As he hit the curve of the island at fifty miles an hour, the hired boat's driver had kicked his rudder hard and amid the shrieks of his three passengers the boat skidded sideways for over a hundred feet. It was what the passengers were paying for. The wave set in motion by the boat hit Panther where he stood frozen to the spot. The wild skidding and quick recovery of the speedy, agile craft brought it to within a hundred feet of Panther and for a moment he didn't know what to do. Then as the driver cut back on the throttle and the roar softened slightly, Panther broke into a lope, fleeing toward the small hammock's shore nearby.

One of the passengers on the boat saw Panther first, even though his seat was lower than the driver's. As the boat rocked to a stable position and the engine was cut back to an idle, the three passengers and the driver all stood and called out to each other as Panther ran in one splashing bound after another until he was lost in the heavy growth that came down to the water's edge. At a little less than half speed, the driver worked his airboat around the hammock until he determined that the cat would lay up there for at least a day or two. *"We scairt him good,"* he mused aloud. *"He sure was scairt pretty good."* The driver of the airboat was sixteen years old.

An hour later the boy deposited his passengers back at the edge of the highway and collected two dollars from each of them. *"Y'all come back, heah?"* he called after them and ran up the dirt path to the shack where he lived with his mother. He gave her the six dollars, took his rifle from under his bed and headed back out onto the wooden boardwalk to where his airboat was loosely hitched.

At full speed he traveled the three miles out to Little Owl Island but cut back to less than quarter speed as he approached. There was no possible way he could approach the island without being heard, not in an airboat, but there was no sense in making any more racket than was absolutely necessary, he reasoned. Still, he knew the cat was at that moment digging in deeper, moving into the deepest mass of vegetation it could find. He reasoned that it would be twenty-four hours at the very least, and possibly much longer, before the badly frightened cat would move out onto any really exposed ground. Even the boy could appreciate how terrifying an apparition his boat must have been to a secretive cat taken by surprise far from cover.

After circling halfway around Little Owl Island, the boy cut hard to port and aimed for a slit barely visible in the overhanging trees and brush. As he approached he cut back to idle and let the boat's momentum carry it through the opening and into the small pool beyond. The brush grabbed at him as he burst through what seemed to be a solid wall of vegetation and his shirt was covered with bits and pieces of leaves and broken twigs.

Once floating in the pool, he cut the engine and let his boat bob and rock until the waves he had created repeated themselves into oblivion. He reached up overhead and grabbed a branch and began working his boat over toward a small open area beside the pool. Pulling along from branch to branch, he finally had the bow of the boat against the land. Stepping down from his high pilot's seat, he jumped ashore and easily manhauled his boat until half of it was beached and dry. He took his rifle from the shelf under his seat and checked the chamber. A single shiny .30–30 cartridge lay there, awaiting his command. By an extraordinary combination of mechanical and chemical ingenuity, mankind had given this sixteen-year-old boy enormous power in the extension of self that is every weapon, every tool. This boy, bronzed, lean, clean and strong for his age, could in a moment be transformed into something else altogether. By the simple willful act of flexing one finger, because of the power granted him by his rifle, this boy with soft blue eyes set in an open, honest and well-tanned face could reach out at 2,410 feet per second and slam one hundred and fifty grains of pointed metal into a target with 1,930 foot-pounds of energy. It was a staggering, even an obscene extension of human power and human will whereby this barefoot boy could narrow his eyes and transform himself into a killer with the powers of Thor by the simplest of acts, the very least of exertions.

It was steaming hot in the airless little pocket that contained the pool. The boy sat with his knees drawn up, sweat pouring down his back. He knew he would have to sit still for an hour at least before beginning to move around on the five-acre island. The noise he had made coming in would have alerted the cat and there was no sense looking for him until an hour or more of silence created an illusion of security. After a while the boy unbuttoned his blue work shirt that had had the sleeves torn off at the shoulders, but still the sweat ran and he finally slipped out of it altogether. He was already barefoot and barelegged halfway to his knees, where his Levi's had been torn off long ago. He sat there, staring down into the pool as long as he could, and then stood, pulled his pants off, stalked out to the end of the airboat and dove. He knew from experience that the alligators that had once bred there had long since been hunted out by poachers and as a native of the Glades he gave little thought to that which would have most bothered a stranger to Little Owl. Certainly there were cottonmouths around, but natives seldom think about them. What they do to avoid them they do automatically and they don't live in constant fear of an encounter.

The pool was nowhere more than seven feet deep, but that was enough and the naked youngster cavorted like a porpoise one minute, like an otter the next. He had been born to a world of calm water and although he had been terrified by the ocean less than fifty miles away the one time in his life he had been taken to it, these waters, whose secrets he knew, contained nothing that frightened him, nothing, even, to cause concern.

He floated on his back, he dived to the bottom in a test of his ability to hold his breath, he arched over and over with his bare bottom getting more air than his lungs. Like the free, wild animal that he was, he claimed one half hour out of the history of the universe; he claimed it as his own, declared it a time for his own sensuousness and joy of self and life. Then he came ashore and stood dripping on the abbreviated ten feet or so of shore left beside his beached boat. He thought a moment and then stretched out flat on his back and stared straight up at the sky as it appeared in patches between the overhanging branches. He stared up and let his mind cavort from fantasy to fantasy. He was prolonging the moment as long as possible. In all the world of hedonistic pleasures, there are few available to a solitary person to equal that of nakedness in a wild place. Nakedness at any time is a challenge to convention and restriction; in a wild place it is something more, it is a denial of time, a reaching back and a fingering of the original fabric of life.

The boy stretched out to his full length and looked around. He could see nests overhead. Some egrets far above flew against the blue toward the west. He could hear birds calling, birds of many kinds, and he could feel the warmth of the earth beneath him, its mother-warmth and its womb-soft power to hold him as he floated suspended in his half-dreams on a lazy afternoon. And the half-dreams of a sixteen-year-old boy for whom solitude is natural can be wonderfully, terribly taunting things. But then his wandering eyes reached the heavy growth of a tree older and larger than the rest. Its foliage was thicker, it was higher and its branches, half hidden in the lower light, were heavier than the trunks of most of the trees around.

As the boy explored the tree, moving his half-closed eyes from branch to branch, he was suddenly drawn to a single slight movement. It was impossible for him to determine the source of the disturbance among the leaves, but somehow he knew that this could be neither a squirrel nor a bird. As his eyes widened and adjusted to the light, he began to see or at least imagine an outline. There was the tip of a tail, then leaves, then a few inches of tawny fur, then more leaves. There was a pinkish nose pad, leaves, and then a single eye, a single yellow, hypnotic eye. The boy was electrified, stunned, and he held his position for several seconds before moving. Panther was poised on the branch, watching him, as he had been ever since the boy began pulling his clothes off before heading for the pool. For a moment the boy was even more embarrassed by the eye of a cat than he would have been by the eyes of a man. That single yellow eye floating in the matrix of the tree gave witness to his shame and he screwed his eyes tight against his image of himself.

Slowly the boy gathered his wits, rolled over onto his stomach and stared back at the cat in the tree. He drew his knees up under him as he braced with his elbows. He inched backwards as he began to stand and then backed down the slight slope to the boat. He never took his eyes off the cat. He reached out behind him, patting the air, feeling for the bow of his boat, across which he had laid his rifle. Panther stood on his branch. Now the boy could see almost all of him and he noted with apprehension that the cat's tail was lashing. Then, in a single movement, Panther was on the ground beneath the tree, his tail still whipping the air and his ears well back. Naked, figuratively as well as literally, still several feet from the boat and only seven from the cat, unwilling to turn his back or make a precipitous movement that could release the coiled spring, the boy stood, trying not to shake, trying not to exude the smell of fear, although fear at the moment consumed him.

For a minute that seemed like an hour, the boy and the cat stood facing each other across the short stretch of open ground near the small pool. Then, fighting to mask the quaver he knew would be there, the boy spoke to the cat, spoke to him as he would to a dog. *"Easy thar, boy, easy now. Atta boy, easy thar now."* Panther split the boy's sentence into broken words as he spat violently. He hunkered down a little lower, turned his head almost over on its side and spat again each time the boy tried to talk. But somehow, his nakedness forgotten, the boy's nerve held and he stood not moving, although the desire to turn and dive for his rifle was almost unbearable, the desire simply to flee virtually a reflex. But the boy knew that the distance between them was less than a third the total distance the cat could spring if it really wanted to. He could neither run away nor reach his rifle. Any precipitous act could trigger the end. Of this there was no doubt at all in the boy's mind.

Forcing himself, the Glades boy stared into Panther's eyes. The cat spat, snarled menacingly, and spat again. Whatever had prompted Panther to come to observe the boy in the first place, whatever had kept him from turning and sailing off through the trees, once discovered, he was now working out in his hostile display. After several minutes, during which he apparently accomplished his end, Panther took a single step backward, held, took another, turned and dissolved. There was barely a disturbance where the brush opened and closed again around him. The boy stood for another moment and then, instead of turning for his rifle, he sank to his knees. With the simplest of utterances — a regionally characteristic and expressive *"Wheweeee"* — he stared after the cat. He stared — and only then did he begin to shake.

🌿 17 🌿

A SIXTEEN-YEAR-OLD BOY WHO HAS BEEN CHALLENGED BY a mountain lion and frightened half out of his wits is not apt to be silent about his adventure once it is over. Within eighteen hours after Panther had dropped from the tree to threaten him (for that is certainly how it seemed), the boy was back on Little Owl with his uncle and two of his uncle's friends. One of the friends carried a twelve-gauge pump loaded with rifled slugs, the other a .30–30 like the boy's, while his uncle carried a .30–40 that had been converted from an army rifle many years earlier. It was a formidable arsenal to range against a single cat but nowhere near as deadly as the four hounds that strained at their leads as the men jumped ashore and followed the boy to the tree from which Panther had dropped.

The hunters knelt and examined the ground beneath the tree. Panther's pugmarks were still visible in the soft earth. The dogs were led to the tracks and allowed to sniff around, but the trail was cold. Although they showed some interest, they did not burst with the enthusiasm that they would have exhibited over a hot scent.

Working through extremely dense brush, the natural line of retreat of a disturbed or frightened cat, the men, the boy and the dogs tried for another trail. They moved completely around the island and then cut diagonals across it several times. There were a number of cold trails, a number of places where they found old tracks and once, just once, the dogs showed signs of excitement, where they came across the windfall under which Panther had slept. The ground, moist and spongy beneath a light scattering of leaves, still showed the outlines of his body.

But Panther was no longer on Little Owl. And now the boy, his uncle and the friends stood on the shore and looked out across the Glades. Nearby the dogs snuffled around in the brush and worried over a rabbit's nest one of them had uncovered. Only three of them managed to get a baby rabbit to kill and the fourth was acting like a spoiled and petulant child.

Out across the flats, hammocks rose like warm, dark breasts, some smaller ones close in and a number of larger ones on the horizon. In between there would be no trail for hounds. There are no footprints on water and tracks on the wind do not hold their shape. The uncle squeezed the boy's shoulder. "He'll come back. You'll git 'im." For a moment, but just a fleeting moment, the boy wondered if he really wanted to. However, that wasn't the kind of thought one could examine, or ever explain to an uncle who owned four of the best tracking hounds in the southern half of the entire state of Florida.

Panther had crossed the flats as soon as night fell. He had moved down to the shore on the opposite side of the island immediately following the episode with the boy and sat back in some dense brush, waiting for darkness to come. Eventually he slipped under a windfall and slept there for several hours. As night came across the flats he had moved off slowly, carefully listening, carefully searching for any sign of danger before exposing himself out in the open.

Less than twenty minutes after leaving Little Owl he was on another hammock, the nearest one, but it was less than an acre in extent and he crossed to another that was only slightly larger. Again he found it impossible to trust so small a piece of ground and moved on. In the course of the night he touched on six of the small hammocks before coming upon Graveyard Key. There, where the Seminoles had once taken their dead, on a fifty-acre hammock where the mist reached up to touch the Spanish moss, he killed a doe and fed, slept and fed again. The hammock was uninhabited. There weren't even any old hunters' shacks to worry about. The eerie legends that surrounded the haunted island, the thought of the ghosts of dead Indians, were too much for men, even men with guns.

Beneath the ground on which Panther killed, fed and slept lay thirty-seven human bodies. Thirty of them lay on their right sides with their heads toward the west. They had been placed on the surface of the ground and red paint had been poured over them as they stared toward the south. Then a mound had been built up over them from muck carried on woven trays by mourning and chanting Indians. The remaining seven bodies had received different treatment. The heads had been removed and the bodies disarticulated. The flesh had been cut away and deposited elsewhere and the bones placed around in a circle with the seven heads sitting upright in the center. Pottery had been smashed and scattered among the grisly remnants. Here again trays of muck and vegetable debris, thousands of them, had been carried to the spot, amid wailing and chanting, and heaped over the surface burials. Before the mound was completed a panther that had strayed onto the hammock during the night was killed and his body treated as the thirty humans' had been. In a smaller mound off to the side his body too lay deep, splashed with red, cleansed by a long-forgotten ritual. The Indians who had mourned for their human dead had mourned no less loudly for the cat as its mound grew beside the other. And here Panther had come to try again for an established base, a place where he would not be bothered. He cared not at all for all the ghosts on Graveyard Key, for the ghosts of men or the ghosts of cats.

Graveyard Key, actually a hammock and not a key or coastal island at all, was the home of many predators. Some of these, much too small to be seen or even scented by Panther, affected him only in the most oblique manner. Others, larger but not necessarily more formidable to their prey than the smaller to theirs, figured discernibly or even prominently in Panther's habitat and life. Not the least of these was the animal known to science as *Crotalus adamanteus,* the eastern diamondback rattlesnake. One of the largest, most venomous and aggressive of the western hemisphere's sixty-five kinds of rattlesnake, he is easily established as one of the dozen or so most dangerous snakes in the world. The giant Panther was destined to meet that day was five feet two inches long. He was a huge, robust snake, with a distinctive pattern of light-centered, dark diamonds with yellow borders running down his length. His dark head with the pale lines along the side was quick and nervous, for although he was the largest poisonous snake in North America and one of the heaviest in the world, he lived in an apparent state of near-panic for his own safety. His tail was tipped by twelve enclosed segments that constituted his rattle. They represented the twelve sheddings during which his rattle had survived intact and *not* the number of years he had been alive, despite what the stranger inevitably is told by people who live around the Everglades.

No one knows how long rattlesnakes have been on this continent, for a snake's fragile bones do not fossilize well, but it has been established that they were here before either man or panther. And they have learned the lessons of survival well.

There are special qualities in the rattlesnake package that make it a matter of some concern to cats that cross its trail. The rattlesnake, a pit viper, was one of the last snakes to evolve on this planet. It is a complicated animal with an enormously sophisticated mechanism that enables it to carry far longer fangs than the fixed ones of the older cobras and their kin. The two fangs, hollow hypodermic needles, actually, lie folded back along the snake's mouth, enclosed in protective sheaths. When prompted to strike and as the head shoots forward in a stabbing motion, the fangs, sometimes well over a half inch in length, swing down and out and are thrust forward into a victim with startling force. Then, and only then, muscles contract, forcing the venom down through ducts and out through the fangs into the punctured tissue. It is a violent, swift stabbing act. The venom involved, a digestive enzyme as well as a killing fluid, is an immensely complicated combination of amino acids and foreign proteins that few species of living creature fail to react to with sickening speed. It is a hemotoxin, essentially, a poisoner of blood, but woven through its chemical structure are factors that affect the nerves as well. To date, no scientist has been able to adequately describe the chemistry of this yellowish, debris-laden substance.

The snake's method of detection and delivery is no less impressive. It does not strike by sight (nor by sound, since it is deaf, as are all snakes), but by *heat.* Midway between its eyes and its external nostrils are two deep indentations, or pits, that give this group of vipers their common name. These organs are heat detectors, incredibly sensitive devices that make it possible for the animal to detect prey or foe by body temperature alone and to follow it as carefully as a man might with his eyes. The snake automatically knows the length of its own strike, about one third of its body length, and can seldom be tempted into action unless directed to do so by his heat-sensing pits.

All of these qualities, all of this specialized equipment, make the pit viper a special kind of foe. Although as much a hunter as Panther, as much a predatory animal, the snake does not really compete. The prey he takes, the smaller birds and mammals mostly, were only occasionally taken by Panther and then only as a passing, even casual act. Although the two hunters were far apart in their interests and in their respective places within the ecology of the hammock, they were then and always had been bitter enemies. The hysterically nervous snake would almost inevitably strike out at any cat that came within that dangerous arc of two feet and an unengaged panther would with equal near-inevitability stop to kill any snake it could overpower. Both animals waged a constant, violent war of useless death.

On his third day on Graveyard Key, after feeding on the doe for the second time, Panther began to wander. He was looking not only for hunting ranges but a permanent base from which to operate, and a new mate as well. These goals kept him in motion — a seeking, searching motion that was the pattern of his life for as long as it lasted. He moved through the heavy-trunked trees just back from the water's edge, he glided over windfalls and finally leaped easily onto the lowest branch of a monster whose gnarled trunk had seen the centuries roll past. Panther stretched out on the branch, casually licked a spot on his shoulder and yawned mightily. He had fed, he was satisfyingly full, and there were no signs of man to disturb him. The ghosts of cat and men could never make themselves known within the secure walls of his cat world. The feline ritual of comfort and life has no use for such foreign elements and they are permanently barred from their consideration by an intelligence that never evolved far enough to embrace them.

Panther didn't sleep, really, but he dozed and his breathing was soon rhythmic. His contentment was apparent, his ease complete. The warm air that moved gently across the hammock's surface was comforting in itself and all was well with his world.

Below where Panther perched, an eastern cottontail rabbit hopped out into the open after first checking for signs of danger and began nibbling on a preferred shrub that grew near the base of the tree. He was unusually careless, and he was immediately spotted by three hunters who feast regularly on his kind. Panther alone of the three was not interested; he alone was not hunting and he watched with casual interest as the drama unfolded below.

No sooner had the rabbit appeared on open ground than the rattlesnake thrust an S-curve forward and moved out of deep cover to position himself behind a clump of weeds six feet from where the little lagomorph fed. His head was raised slightly off the ground and malevolent eyes focused unblinkingly on his potential victim. The pale forked tongue shot out in rapid flicking movements to gather more information from the chemistry of the wind. Particles of air were carried into the Jacobson's organ in the roof of the snake's mouth with each flick of the tongue and were there analyzed.

But the rattlesnake wasn't the only hunter with an interest in the rabbit. Through the opening in the trees that allowed the sunlight to penetrate to the forest floor, another watched with practiced eyes as she circled for position. Her strike would have to be swift, for her descending body would cast shadows that could alert the rabbit in time for it to escape. The red-tailed hawk, only recently arrived from a northern forest where she had nested and raised her third brood, was hungry and she wanted the rabbit badly enough to drop through the hole in the trees. As an individual bird she preferred open-field hunting, where her approach could be more lateral than vertical, but she was flexible enough, hungry enough, to plunge through the hole that opened up beneath her. Her blue-black beak and her yellow feet armed with their devastatingly powerful black talons could make short work of the little rabbit, but first she had to catch him. As she wheeled and sorted out her position and timing, the sun reflected off her brown back with its zonal barrings of amber, cinnamon, cream, black and white. Her enormous brown eyes with the sharpest of precision sighting studied the details of the scene below, but she missed the snake, who was shielded from above by the overhanging weeds under which he had crawled in the first leg of his hunt. Certain that the timing was right, certain of her trajectory, the hawk dropped. Whether her shadow fell across him sooner than the hawk had reckoned, or whether he heard the sound of the wind in her feathers, the hawk arrived less than two seconds after the rabbit had hopped frantically aside.

Played in slow motion, the action as it unfolded was amazing in the interplay of forces involved. The hawk had dropped and somehow alarmed her prey a second or so too early. In an amazingly swift reflex he leaped and came to earth less than the critical two feet short of where the still undetected rattlesnake was poised, ready to strike. Because the trees surrounding the very small clearing were thick and heavy, the hawk decided not to swoop upward in a single continuous movement but braked to land on the vacated spot near where the rabbit had been feeding. At the same instant the rattlesnake struck. With lightning-like swiftness he embedded his two erect fangs into the rabbit's shoulder and discharged several drops of venom. For a brief instant the rabbit, focus of so much violence, raised his forefeet off the ground as he was quite literally pinned to the snake's head. Then the snake recoiled from its strike. Instantly sickened by the venom, the rabbit tumbled over twice, tried to right himself, tumbled again and managed to crawl under some brush. Within his small body the venom was acting rapidly. The digestive enzymes began breaking tissues down immediately, starting the digestive process that would normally continue in the snake's stomach after he swallowed his prey whole. Massive internal hemorrhages started and progressed inward as the venom invaded the small animal's body. In seconds, no more than that, the rabbit was paralyzed. An involuntary kicking of his hind legs alone showed him to be still alive. His eyes were glazed and his neck, frozen midway in a spasm of pain and fear, was hunched over so that the animal's head appeared to be attached to his body at a crazy angle.

Under more normal circumstances the snake would have given the wildly gyrating, then quickly frozen rabbit a few minutes to die before following his trail, tracking him to where he hid by the scent he laid down. But this was not a normal situation. The red-tailed hawk landed six feet away as the snake recoiled. Himself the potential victim of death-dealing talons from above, the snake immediately drew the back half of his body forward until it coiled under him, drew his head back into a loose S and began to vibrate his tail frantically. Instinctively he had known not to discharge his full dose of venom into the rabbit and he held more than enough in reserve to kill the bird as well, if he could embed his fangs in her feather-protected flesh.

The bird was aware of the snake less than a second before she landed, and immediately hunched herself into her fighting posture with her wings spread and her shoulders thrust forward. The snake's fury was boundless and the bird was no less in flames. On the branch above, Panther had been watching and then, as the bird had plummeted past him, he stood on his branch and followed the action with mounting interest.

The bird stared at the snake with unveiled hatred and the snake vibrated his tail wildly in return. Except for the snake's tail and the pink tongue that appeared in spastic little motions, the action was arrested. Then the bird pushed downward. The tips of her widespread wings trailed in· the dirt and she rose straight up about a foot and then, quite suddenly, was over the snake. Before her talons could grasp the writhing body below her, the snake lashed out and pulsed sideways. It was a convulsive movement, but it worked and the bird came down for the second time on barren ground. Whether or not she was tired from her long flight or suffering from some other factor that slowed her normally sparklike reflexes, twice in a space of seconds she had misjudged. Normally, she would have had the rabbit, for although she was not perfect, she was extremely good at her craft and her percentage of success had been extraordinarily high. Normally, too, she would have killed the snake, for she had killed many before and fed off them. But here again, it was a timing error of a fraction of a second and as she turned to face the newly gathered snake and prepare for a second launch, a numbness appeared in her left shin. It was only momentary; then there was a searing flamelike pain that blossomed there and her leg collapsed. A fang had creased her shin and a drop of venom had been deposited.

Some of it was drawn into the tissue along the line of the fang scratch and there it began its fatal work.

The amount of venom that actually penetrated the bird's tissues would not have been especially serious to a human being whose body weight exceeded seventy-five pounds. It would probably have only sickened such a person. But the bird weighed no more than a few pounds and the one drop of venom was enough. In moments the bird was sick, in minutes she would be dead. She drooped her wings in a gesture that can only be regarded as an approximation of despair. She sank down on the side where the small injury had been delivered and then her other leg collapsed as well. Her wings remained widespread until she finally righted herself and drew them in against her body. With enormous effort she managed to collect herself enough to fly and she came down on a heavy branch just across the clearing from Panther. She would remain on the branch for twenty minutes; then she would fall to earth, unable to hang on any longer. She would die on the way down as her heart hemorrhaged and came to a violent, slushing stop.

Panther, whose world was violence and who knew well the meaning of death, was lathered into a kind of hypnotic rage by the action below. The rabbit, the snake, the hawk, all moved with speed and suddenness. It was stimulating beyond his power to endure. He dropped to earth and stood before the snake, just out of his reach. The snake was now in an even greater fury than before. His head lay flat along the S-curve where it rose above his tightly coiled body. His rattle kept up a constant drumming *hummm* that expressed the animal's attitude precisely. Nearby, the rabbit, the original focus of it all, lay dead. Nearby the hawk perched, dying. The snake and the panther were alone in the ring. Panther feinted, tentatively reaching out with his front right paw. The snake lashed. The strike was short and the snake withdrew toward the whirring buzz of his own tail, and Panther feinted again. Again the snake lashed out ineffectively.

Three, four, five times the battle-wise cat drew the snake's lashing strike. On the sixth pass the snake's body hit the ground with a hard plunk. He was tiring and he withdrew with less speed than before, repositioned his head with less precision. But infuriated beyond all containing, he twisted his body forward several inches without significantly altering his posture. Panther took a single step backward and reached out again tentatively with his right paw. Seven, eight, nine times the cat tempted the snake in his useless exertions. Ten, eleven, twelve times the snake struck short of the cat, who stood with his ears laid back and his lips curled upward. Then the snake slowly lowered his head to his top coil and would not strike again. His tail still whirred on, but with less conviction somehow. The snake was tired; the amount of tension he had withstood was more than even his powerful muscles could bear indefinitely.

Twice Panther eased closer to the snake, who continued to watch with eyes of hate, and twice the lanceolate head rose slightly off the diamond-marked top coil. But then Panther moved, lightning-like, the action too swift to follow. The snake was writhing in a number of convulsive knots. He was turning in upon himself with his ventral scales as often apparent as his dorsal. His back was broken in two places and his neck was bitten through. There was blood on his scales and raw meat was exposed. He was only moments from death.

And Panther was recoiling, backing up on three legs, rapidly shaking his right front foot, shaking it as if to rid himself of the venom the snake had managed to inject into his heel pad as a final gesture. Panther's heel pad was momentarily numb; then the flames started, the searing pain at the wound site. Panther had been struck by a dying snake who had nothing at all for which to save his precious drops of venom. Panther, who had had nothing to do with the fight below, who, well fed as he was, had had no vested interest in the rabbit, the snake or the hawk, could not resist. Panther, whose cat personality had drawn him into the fray, would limp away as the pain reached for his hock and crawled toward his cat's soul.

🌿 18 🌿

OF ALL THE WOUNDS PANTHER WAS EVER TO RECEIVE IN
his life, this, although one of the smallest, was the most serious. One of the dying snake's fangs had hooked into the heel
pad of his right front foot. True, the fang had broken off in the
action, but before it did a quantity of venom, just about all the
snake had left after his unusually active day, had been discharged. Almost half of it had been injected into the small
puncture wound before the violent action tore the fang away.
It would have been more than enough to kill a smaller animal,

but Panther was a full-grown mountain lion and his body weight and his ability to accept and tolerate noxious foreign proteins were sufficient for his survival. It was, however, a narrow margin.

The pain had begun immediately. It was searing hot one instant, freezing cold the next, as the nerve endings in the area were assaulted by forces that had not affected them before. Immediately below the surface of the pad, the bleeding started and was soon so profound that the area became severely distended. Within two hours the entire paw was so swollen that its former outline could hardly be discerned. Within four hours the cat was crippled. In the hours that followed, the swelling reached all the way to his ribs and there great sores formed that would soon erupt and ooze. His leg was a solid paralyzed mass and no joints functioned. They barely showed. On the second day, as his chest, neck and face began to swell, the gross swelling of his lower leg began to go down. He was hungry and violently thirsty, but he continued to lay up. He refused to move; at times he seemed to stop breathing. From time to time he exhaled small groaning sounds. The agony that went with his physical distortion was plain to see.

The swelling retreated rapidly once it started down, but necrotic tissue formed at the original wound site and around several of the erupted sores on his side. Eventually the black, evil-smelling areas on his side healed, leaving large scars, but the tissue around the point of the fang's momentary entry did not do as well. When Panther was next able to put his foot down on the ground, it was without a heel pad. A raw excavation remained where the entire gangrenous heel pad had finally sloughed away. In a very real way the snake had marked him for life. His track was now immediately discernible, distinctly different from that of any other mountain lion in the entire state of Florida. The poorest tracker that would ever cross his trail would now know him instantly from the mark he made.

At the end of eight days, a period during which he had managed to crawl to water several times but during which he had not fed, Panther had suffered a dramatic weight loss. Before he could seek food and eat again, he would lose a full third of his normal weight. Most of that was lost in those eight pain- and fever-filled days.

After ten days, when he was almost too weak to crawl out of hiding and down to water, Panther managed to take a frog. Before the day was out he managed to take a dozen more and then spent hours catching insects. He survived on this meagerest of fare until he was able to overpower a young and very inexperienced raccoon. From there he went on to slightly larger prey, but it would be fully six months before he would take a deer again.

An argument has existed longer than man can recall concerning the capacity of dumb animals to experience pain and fear. There can be no doubt that Panther felt pain most profoundly during the worst hours of the venom's grip on him. He licked his foot endlessly and a general rawness was added to the specific sore. He was, in fact, in agony for days and this alone was almost enough to kill him. It certainly contributed to his weight loss. As for fear, there can be little doubt that he felt that profoundly as well. While the cat doesn't link things together as a man does, he does have emotional reactions to the things that happen within his ken. Panther could not understand that the snake had venom or that the snake's action was a legitimate one of self-defense. He could not even hate the snake for hurting him. He was also incapable of fearing death as a specific, for that fear would presuppose an awareness of both life and self and that is far too sophisticated for the feline brain to accomplish. However, within these roughly under- stood restrictions, Panther feared and hurt and he would be a wiser cat in the end. Never again in his life would he fail to skirt the first hint of a rattlesnake's warning buzz.

It was time to wander once more. Although he still limped slightly, he had quickly learned to accommodate himself to his missing heel pad. It was tender but no longer as inflamed as it had been, or sick with necrotic tissue. He was hunting again and gaining weight. He was also beginning to feel the need for a new mate. The essential cat inside of him had come through intact.

Violence and trauma had surgically severed him from every firm base he had ever established. His mother's suddenly vi- cious intolerance had ended his seemingly secure hold on Billy Buck. The old man and Dora had torn apart his next little world, on Bitterroot. Then there had been the boy, then the snake. Now Panther was wandering again. In time he was hunting deer, in time he was back at his top weight and in time he met and took an inexperienced female. He had to cripple a younger male to do it, but Panther was no longer a cat that could be driven off by bluff or a cat likely to lose a fight. The two seasons of the Everglades came and went in their rhythm of wet and dry.

Panther's cubs were born beneath a windfall on a hammock he never visited. He would never know them as his own when he would occasionally cross their trail in the years ahead. Again he mated, again his cubs were born and Panther's years were full upon him. He weighed very close to two hundred pounds. He was experienced now in all things — man, animals and weather. He knew fire and water, wind and mates. He was a trophy-sized cat that had by a series of what can only be called miracles survived to be larger, older and wiser than ninety percent of all the cats that were born in the Everglades during his lifetime.

Panther held back in the deep cover until the light failed and the fireflies began blinking along the water's edge. The slough was deep and quite wide and there was no place where he could wade across. It would be a swim, a strenuous one, and he would be exposed all the way across. Darkness was the minimum protection he could accept. By some strange combination of stimuli that we call thinking in animals, Panther had decided to move across to the hillier hammock on the other side of the slough. Once that determination was established he had to go.

There were several small alligators in the slough but none large enough to molest a full-grown panther. The cottonmouth water moccasin that normally hunted the slough was across and downstream, digesting a particularly large duckling. So, without interference, he made it across. He pulled himself out on the sloping bank opposite and shook himself again and again. His fur was not water-repellent and he looked ragged and used as he tried to shed the excess moisture. It was dark by then and it would take him some time to dry out. It would have been quicker in sunlight, to be sure, but far more hazardous, or at least nerve-wracking, for a supercautious cat.

After several minutes of attending to his coat he began casting around for signs of prey. He had been living off smaller animals for weeks and deer was what he craved. It didn't take him long to pick up a trail. In the moonlight a small buck had passed by, stopped to nibble on some browse that grew almost at the water's edge, and then moved off into an open parklike area back from the shore.

Panther, by luck, had come ashore within a hundred yards of where the buck stood. Somehow the deer missed the sounds the cat made as he came ashore. The winds were in Panther's favor and he was able to come up to a point just across the small open glade. He hunkered down behind a bush and watched and waited. He crouched with his forepaws extended. His head lay between them and the only signs of life he gave were the shallow dips in his rib cage and the small flicks of the end of his tail. These were the gentlest of oscillating movements, but they expressed the cat's mood perfectly.

Panther had a fix on the buck that was almost perfect. He could see the animal's occasional head movements and the spastic little flickings of its ears in the bright moonlight. He had the deer's scent and he could hear the small thumps as the nervous animal periodically lifted its hoof and dropped it again. But still Panther waited.

When, somehow, Panther had satisfied himself that the buck was not going to come his way, he began to move himself. Hugging the ground and taking advantage of every bit of cover there was to be had, he drifted noiselessly toward his

prey. The deer, designed by nature to be completely aware of
his surroundings at all times, equipped to test, retest and eval-
uate everything that happens anywhere near him, for some
reason was not keen enough to sense the ghostlike cat that was
drifting toward him.

Then the signal came. From somewhere the warning
reached the buck and his head shot up. His tail flicked, exposing its white underside, and his muscles tensed for flight. In a
second, two at the most, he would have made his escape. But
he had waited that extra second too long. At almost the same
instant both Panther and the buck began moving at full speed.
Panther burst out of his cover at a gallop. In the first instant,
capitalizing on the initial thrust of his hindquarters as they
drove him out of his crouch, his forelegs were fully extended
out in front, his hind legs out to the rear. In the next, his four
legs were bunched under him to gather up more yards and
provide even greater thrust. It was a heart-bursting explosion
of energy and Panther was capable of maintaining it for only a
matter of seconds. He had been gathering his energy and his
determination for this supreme moment of the kill and he had
to make it pay off almost instantly. Even his great heart, even
his powerful muscles, couldn't keep it going beyond the initial
charge.

The deer reacted in blind panic. The cat had exploded out of
the brush so close at hand that there was no time for anything
but an immediate physical response. Even the meager mental
faculties the buck had at his disposal could not be brought into
play. There just wasn't time.

In the blindness of his panic the buck broke toward a bar-
rier of bushes that was too high for even him to clear, magnifi-

cent jumper though he was. He veered toward a second avenue of escape, the one he should have selected in the first place. That split second of hesitation was all that Panther needed. It was what he had been depending on and he hit the buck so hard that they were both carried into the bushes beyond by the shock of impact. Branches smacked at Panther's face as he rode the startled buck to ground and he was half buried in leaves and stems as he leaped forward on his prey and reached for the neck. He had caught the buck a foot too far back and had his fangs embedded in the animal's shoulder, where they would be relatively ineffective.

Panther's right paw shot forward and his fully extended claws hooked deeply into the buck's nose. It was an easy matter for Panther to force the deer's head back and the sound of the neck breaking was clearly audible as Panther simultaneously raked into the buck's exposed throat with the claws on his left forepaw and his teeth reached the base of the wildly struggling animal's skull. The entire action had taken less than ten seconds. It was a clean, even a merciful kill. In a way it was a necessary one. The buck was able to reproduce himself; he had come of age. Since he had been unable to detect the panther's approach and had blundered in his efforts to escape, the genetic pool of the local deer population could well do without his incomplete potential. He was probably an inferior deer to begin with. There were better ones around to sire the new crops of deer young yet to be born.

Panther lay across his kill for fully fifteen minutes before settling down to feed. He panted his way through the first ten until his heartbeat rate, body temperature and other processes settled down from the enormous peak they had reached to facilitate the kill. It takes a surging infusion of chemicals into the bloodstream and tissues of an animal to enable it to burst from a relatively stationary position into top speed without any period of buildup. It takes an explosive change in character to convert an animal from a hidden, cautious creature one moment into an exposed and totally committed killer the next. The deer has hooves and the buck has antlers. Cats whose commitments are less than total can be killed by either. Panther needed the time he lay panting across his prey to recover from the shock of his own conversion, from the impact of his own energy.

After he had fed, Panther raked a few leaves across the buck in a token cacheing ritual and moved down to the water's edge to drink. He crouched down and had barely begun to drink when something further along the shore caught his attention. Another cat was coming ashore after taking the long swim across the wide slough. Panther listened and then drifted back into cover. He began moving along the hammock parallel with the channel that ran just off its shore. The signal was not long in coming to him. The new arrival was a female ready to breed and Panther homed in on his new mate. She would be his fourth, the third that would bear his cubs.

⚜ 19 ⚜

MOST OF PANTHER'S EARLIER WANDERINGS HAD BEEN within the boundaries of Dade County north of U. S. Route 41, better known to tourists as the Tamiami Trail. On a few occasions he wandered north into Broward County and hunted there. Once, at two in the morning, he had actually crossed the Trail itself and moved westward into Monroe County, into Everglades National Park. He recrossed the park boundary again within forty-eight hours.

Now, in his fifth year, he was in the western part of Dade

County again, moving west on about the same latitude as North Miami. He was just a little over twenty-eight miles west of Miami Beach, but he might as well have been on a different planet. Twenty-eight miles away the women wore mink to breakfast and men constructed the most elaborate swimming pools in the world within inches of some of the finest beaches on earth. Neither men nor women swam in either pool or ocean, but the card games were marathon affairs. Cadillacs were the Fords of the land and a woman thought herself naked if she didn't own and travel with at least five wigs. But the area those few miles to the west where Panther stalked was something else. Here snakes and alligators could threaten his life, here he would fight to the death for a mate and here the hungry hunted around the clock and the prey animals shrank in terror before the onslaught. The evil and the primeval were never closer together. Two ways of life were never further apart.

His westward course eventually carried Panther across into Collier County and then he cut toward the northwest. Some nights later he was due west of the Florida State Seminole Indian Reservation and there he found his fifth mate. He lingered in the area for several days, in a small, tight little forest that grew up out of dry land, and then he took a deer. It was the first time he had ever spent any time away from the world of water and he was exploring the possibilities of the area when the trouble began. He had taken to hunting in broad daylight as a result of several months without close human contact and had perhaps become a little careless. Old Tommy (he was the most ancient Seminole in the area and no one knew any other name for him) saw the cat working along a canal, trying to trap an otter out in the open. He carried the story home with him that night.

The news of the panther that had wandered into the area made its way around the settlement and the next morning several boys went out to check the soft soil along the canal boundary. The place where the tracks appeared was only six miles south of where Cuth Wallen had his horse spread, so a call was made to warn the breeder that he might be having trouble in the nights ahead. With thanks to the caller, Cuth assured him that he would be alert and keep dogs and rifle handy. No horse breeder is ever likely to forget the early range stories in which ranchers claimed that it was quite literally impossible to rear colts in mountain-lion country until *all* of the cats had been cleared out. This claim, and perhaps there was a measure of truth in it, seemed to justify the slaughter of thousands of mountain lions all across America. That isn't hard to understand when it is remembered that men were hung for stealing horses.

Although Panther had crossed horse trails a few times in his wanderings and had paused to puzzle over the strange scent that always hung there, he had never been close to a horse before and had certainly never seen one. As he moved northward through the pocket forest, he crossed trails where horses traveled regularly and where dung was scattered all around. The horse smell, heavy in the warm, humid air, was more powerful than he had ever known it to be and he became more and more interested as he moved forward. Several times he traveled on the trails themselves but inevitably became nervous after a few minutes and struck off to travel instead through heavy cover. Panther did not like the feeling of being exposed on all sides. The longer he was in the open, the more nervous he became. He was an eastern mountain lion, a panther of forested land.

As he moved north toward the Cuth Wallen spread, he became strangely excited. Ghostlike, he seemed to be moving sideways in time toward another kind of life, a more dangerous one than he had ever known. For the first time in his life Panther had had his move announced in advance — the phone call had anticipated him — and for the first time in his life he was closing in on domestic animals. No more damning thing can be said about a wild predator; nothing creates quite the same reaction in man, nothing triggers quite the same anger and determination. Although man often treats his livestock with staggering brutality, he becomes strangely sentimental when a challenge to their welfare comes from without.

The sense of excitement that gripped the great cat as he dissolved his way through the dense growth mounted as he moved. He slipped in and out of patches of moonlight that occasionally found their way to earth through the heavy growth overhead, treading softly from a world of relative security toward one of extreme danger. The guns that would level at him at every turn would not acknowledge his past struggles to survive, would not recognize him as a living member of a wild community with certain duties to perform. He would be a panther, a wildcat in horse country, where the tradition of hate for wildcats has always been maintained with the fervor of a religion.

It was still dusk when he came to the end of the trees and saw the flat pasture open out before him. The elevation for miles around was uniformly ten feet above sea level and there were few distinguishable features in the land. What trees there were out in the open were distant and thinly spaced. It was pasture land, range land, sacred, fenced, patrolled and protected. It was a ranch where horses were bred, Arabian horses. Here a hoofed animal would not be a nameless white-tailed deer but a registered horse whose potential was being watched and depended upon and whose worth was likely to be in the thousands of dollars.

The horse scent was everywhere. Horsehairs were tangled in the wires of the fence and caught on every detail of the fence posts. The ground was littered for miles around with horse manure and for dozens of years horse urine had soaked the ground. The turf was scored with a million hoofprints where the animals had raced and roamed, cavorted and pranced. Never had Panther been in a place where the odors were so strong, so clear and so totally pervasive. Heady from the smell, drawn compellingly by it, he moved out from the trees and stood next to a fence post, staring out across the field. The moon slipped through black fingers of clouds and splashed the ground with irregular shapes at equally irregular intervals. Panther was tense, for somehow he sensed that all might not be well. But still the heady smell drew him forward and he stepped past the post, ducked under the wire and was in the pasture, on private property for the first time in his life. Off in the distance a dog barked and another howled in return. A hundred yards ahead a barn owl swooped low like a giant moth and then dropped on a rat that had revealed itself to her superb night eyes. Nearby, bats flitted erratically, snatching insects up by the hundreds. Some of their frenetic squealings were audible to Panther, but he had other matters to occupy him.

There were no horses in the immediate area and Panther started out across the field. For three nights, ever since the phone call, the horses had been herded in at dusk and were penned up three quarters of a mile away. Near where they stood behind their slatted wooden barriers, dozing their night away, dogs were staked out at measured intervals. In a pickup truck parked nearby, men sat and smoked and cursed the cat that was costing them their sleep. Rifles and spotlights were at hand, and so was the determination to rid the land of every last cat once and for all.

But Panther had emerged from the woods considerably east of the holding pens and would come nowhere near the trap that was awaiting him there. However, even this eventuality had been anticipated by the professionals who had been hired within an hour of the phone call, and a trap of a different sort had been laid.

Panther heard the noise moments after he crossed over into the pasture. He heard it because a goat had sensed him and had begun to bleat. Panther crouched lower, unable to appreciate that the animal he was stalking would wait for him because he had no other choice. He moved in a semicircle, tested all winds and remained alert for signs of danger. He closed in and with an easy rush killed the bleating kid. He lay across his kill for several minutes and then fed from one of its hindquarters. He tried to carry his victim off to a more sheltered area but was stopped by the rope around its neck. With nothing nearby that could be scraped across the carcass, he left it where it lay and headed back into the forest. Two hundred yards beyond the tree line, he stopped and lay up to wash his fur and sleep. All had gone well; it had all been very simple, disarmingly simple — as was the intent of Cuth Wallen and the hunters he had hired. All in fact had gone as planned.

The ranch hand riding one of Cuth Wallen's utility horses made the circuit of the staked goats just as the sun was first tinting the east. He found Panther's kill and spotted the unmistakable cat pugs at the second station he checked, and raced madly back toward the ranch house. Within forty-five minutes a pickup truck worked its way along the bumpy road that ran southward along the eastern boundary of the pasture a quarter of a mile east of where Panther had made the goat kill. It stopped on a signal from the mounted ranch hand who rode alongside. The hunters dropped the tailgate and began untying the thongs that held the five hounds in the truck's well. One by one the dogs were allowed to jump to the ground and were led to where the goat lay dead and partially eaten.

The cat trail was still hot and the dogs registered their excitement almost immediately. The hunters spoke encouragingly to the dogs and let them lead off while still holding the leather straps that were fastened to their collars. As the dogs pulled and strained along the trail directly toward the woods, one hunter nodded and said, "They'll tree him in there for sure." The leashes were unhitched and the five hounds burst loose, tearing toward the wood, voicing their excitement in round notes that rolled and tumbled across the early morning land. They tore through patches of ground mist, they cleared the fence easily by ducking low without changing pace and then burst across the boundary that marked the forest. The hunters were not far behind, but they didn't have to worry. No cat fleeing before five large and noisy hounds will stay on the ground for long. Once it treed they would never let it down. They would hold it at bay until the hunters arrived, all the while working themselves into a wild fury as they tried to scale the tree after the cat themselves.

The seemingly instinctive dread panthers have of the sounds dogs make may go back to times when there were more panthers and more wolves. Perhaps there is an elemental hatred between the two. This is often suggested, but it has never been proved.

Panther heard the dogs even before they reached the fence and he was on his feet. A low moaning filled his throat and he moved out from under the windfall and stood for just a moment to be sure of the direction. Then, in a single bounding leap, he cleared the enormous tree and crashed through the thick brush beyond. Moving as rapidly as the heavy growth would allow — and he was now staying strictly in heavy growth — he pushed on into the woods away from the field. But although he could leap further and negotiate more difficult individual obstacles than the dogs could ever manage, they could eventually force their way through any country the cat could choose. Although he pushed as hard as he could, the gap between the single fleeing cat and the five yowling hounds began to close. A wildcat does not need much stamina in the ordinary course of events and can be easily winded. For dozens of generations stamina was one of the ingredients bred into the hounds. Long after any wildcat had dropped from exhaustion, these genetically engineered dogs would still be pressing on. Stamina was in their blood, in their fibres, in their hearts.

After fifteen minutes of flight the distance between Panther and his pursuers was closed by nearly thirty yards. The dogs were gaining minute by minute and the volume of their yowling carried this message clearly to the now thoroughly terrified cat. When the dogs were no more than thirty yards behind him, Panther spotted a huge tree and in one leap landed nearly twenty feet up on its trunk. Climbing furiously, he was soon forty feet above the ground and moving out onto a heavy limb. The debris kicked loose from the bark was still drifting down when the dogs arrived at the bottom of the tree and began hurling themselves against it in a frenzy of pursuit and determination. Eight, even ten feet they leaped in an effort to reach the panther so far above their heads. Their howling intensified. A quarter of a mile away three men followed the sounds of the hounds at an easy jog. With a reasonable amount of caution for where they stepped, this being ideal snake country, they pushed on with an experienced and certain ease. In ten minutes they stood under the tree, staring up at the cat and smiling at the display their volatile hounds were putting on. Cuth Wallen had offered them five hundred dollars for the cat if it could be proven that it had actually crossed over onto his ranch land. Panther's pugmark near the slaughtered goat was like a signature on the bottom of a death warrant. He was now worth five hundred dollars dead or alive and three men, three guns and five hounds waited below.

⚘ 20 ⚘

PANTHER GLARED DOWN AT HIS PURSUERS AND TWICE
moved over closer to the trunk. The hounds below, leaping as
they were, made him nervous and he moved out again each
time, out as far as he dared go on the heavy but nonetheless
sagging branch. Nearly two hundred pounds out on the end of
the limb applied enormous pressure and it looked to the men
below as if the branch might snap.

There were many other heavy trees in the area but none
near enough for Panther to jump to. The nearest branch that

could have taken his weight was nearly forty feet away, the nearest trunk over fifty. His tree was an island and on it he was exposed.

It would have been an easy shot. Any one of the three men could have backed off a dozen feet to avoid the awkwardness of shooting straight up and had their cat in profile, stationary at less than fifty feet.

The dogs continued their clamorous yowling and wailing and the three men lit up to talk things over. One of them sat down with his back to the trunk, ignoring the angry wildcat that poised over his head.

"Ole Grunt up there at the gas station lost his cat some time back. Figgers it was a good draw. Reckon he'd go twenty-five bucks for this 'un."

"Might go higher. He's a lot bigger'n the one he had."

"Awful lota trouble to go to for twenty-five bucks!"

"Hell, I don' care. I'll go on up affer him."

"OK with me. You?"

"Hell, no fun in jes shootin' him, sittin' up there like that."

And so it was decided. Panther was not to be executed but captured alive and sold to Ole Grunt, who owned the gas station with the roadside zoo on the new County Road. Grunt's last panther, bought from hunters as a six-month-old cub, had lived nearly two years, a record for Grunt's animals. Hovering in its own filth in a cage so small that it couldn't even stand up properly, the miserable, half-starved creature had actually survived for twenty-two months. Grunt's last black bear had lasted only six. No bobcat had survived there more than a year. His snakes did somewhat better, generally, but still none lasted very long. Grunt hated his animals for the extra work they caused him. On several occasions, when he returned to his gas station late at night after an evening at the roadhouse a dozen miles down the highway, he had so severely beaten several of them that they died before dawn. He was cruel when sober, vicious beyond belief when drunk. Grunt hated his animals, but they were an attraction. As in so many areas of the country, the sign ROADSIDE ZOO drew bored and weary travelers who had to buy their gas somewhere anyway. Collectively, they support one of the cruelest uses to which our wildlife can be put. This was the future the hunters envisioned for Panther.

Will, one of the two younger men, hooked the loops of rope into his belt and with a heave from his brother and uncle made it up onto the first branch. From there, with a little caution, he made it up onto the next one, and then the next. In less than five minutes he was five feet below Panther, who was glaring down at the intruder and spitting with all the hatred he could muster. As the agile young man began reaching up to grasp the branch on which Panther stood, the wildly enraged and thoroughly frightened cat moved further out onto his branch and lifted his right paw as if to slap out, as if to rake his opponent with his powerful claws.

Finally Will made it onto Panther's branch and pressed himself back against the trunk of the tree so as not to add his weight to that of the cat's; the branch was already bent at a precarious angle. He began unlimbering the rope from his belt and shaking out the loop he would need to encircle the cat's head. Panther was further enraged by the man's movements and by the vibrations that ran down the branch to him from where the man sat. He adjusted his position to accommodate his movements.

The hounds below kept up their yowling and the two men watched carefully with their guns ready. But they were not needed. Panther was thoroughly intimidated and would not charge the man who shared his trembling perch with him. The dogs had done their work well.

Will flipped the loop experimentally at Panther several times. The rope hit the cat in the face, but his paw was quicker and the loop was easily deflected. Still, Will knew from experience that sooner or later he would have the cat's head or paw in the loop and from there on it would be routine. Once snagged, even the largest panther is easily trussed — not easily, perhaps, but no real problem for an experienced hand.

Several more times the loop flicked toward Panther and each time, whether or not it touched him or just came close, his right paw went up in the same defensive gesture. It was these gestures, these characteristic and individual movements, Will was judging. Once he knew them well enough, he would know how to take his cat. The fact that he faced the cat over a stretch of limb no more than eight feet long didn't bother him a bit. The cat was exposed to his brother and uncle below and their rifles. But he knew the cat wouldn't charge. He had once seen his father club one to unconsciousness in a tree without the cat even making a pass at the man.

Each time the loop came close Panther altered his position on the branch. Each time he brought his paw back down he had to move slightly to keep his balance. The strain was too much, although the fact was not yet apparent to the man above or the men below. Finally the first hint came. There was a cracking sound and the part of the branch where Panther stood dropped six inches. White wood began to show through cracks in the brownish-gray bark near the trunk. The cracks widened and the end of the branch dropped another six inches. Panther could feel the hazardous dipping and began climbing up the branch toward where Will was sitting. Again the branch dipped lower and Will suddenly was faced with the sight of a huge male mountain lion inching his way up the branch toward where he sat involved with his loops and knots. The dipping of the branch had brought side stems heavily laden with leaves between Panther and the men below. They could no longer see his outline distinctly. They no longer had a clear shot.

The final break came as Panther leaped at the trunk of the tree. He hit it only inches from where Will had been crouching. The young man's body fell crashing through the branches below. He fought desperately to grab something on the way down, but he didn't have a chance. The men below heard his head strike a heavy branch. What they couldn't hear was the sound his neck made as it broke. Will's brother and uncle knelt over him and called his name and patted his face, though they both knew he was dead. Will's brother, whose eighteenth birthday was the following day, was sobbing. The two boys had been identical twins.

The dogs were momentarily distracted by Will's body crashing to earth and in that instant Panther hit the ground on the opposite side of the tree and cleared a fourteen-foot-high windfall at full speed. He had started slipping down the trunk backwards as soon as the branch let go. This was to be his one chance.

The dogs took several moments to recover and realize what had happened. All but one of them broke after the cat in wild cry and disappeared into the brush. The one dog that remained behind, Will's special pet, a large and wise-faced tan bitch, was sniffing around his body and whining until the boy's brother finally pushed her away. She lay down nearby and waited.

Panther, still thoroughly terrified, kept up his full pace as he cleared the highest and densest obstacles he could find. Whenever he encountered a fallen tree he ran along its trunk, forcing the dogs with their less certain feet to do the same. Now he had two distinct advantages: the wisest dog in the pack, the old tan bitch, was not with the hunt, and all the time the cat had been in the tree the dogs had been leaping about below. They were now tired, despite their built-in stamina, and Panther was relatively fresh.

After about half a mile Panther hit a stream and instead of leaping across it jumped into its middle and doubled back under some overhanging brush. He worked his way along in the water for about a hundred yards and then came ashore behind the dogs as they yapped and howled on down toward the stream. With an easy leap Panther made the first branch of a heavy tree and moved out twenty-five feet to its end. He jumped to earth there and moved off at a right angle to his original track, the one the dogs had followed. In the meantime they were fussing and fuming along the bank of the stream, trying to find some sign. Ten minutes later, when one of them finally found the spot where Panther had come ashore, Panther was well over a mile away, still treeing himself at intervals, still cutting his track into chunks and still making use of every hazard nature provided. Within an hour after it started, the second chase was over and the four dogs were making their confused way back to where Will had died. Later that day a friend of the family's would come out to collect them. He would find them lying dejectedly beneath the tree, still unaware of what had happened.

As the moon slipped behind a pile of dirty clouds, Panther ventured out into the open. He stopped to test the air, to test the wind, to seek any secrets the night might hold. Satisfied at last that it was safe to move, he stepped down off the dry ground and began wading across the saw-grass flats, toward the southeast, toward country he knew, a land of water where human exploitation was still at a minimum. A half hour later he came ashore on a small hammock and moved back up from the shore. Overhead an owl swooped low, looking for prey. Off in the distance he could hear a frantic thumping and snorting mixed with the enraged *whirrr* of a ground rattler. Behind a screen of brush, over beyond a small alligator pool, a white-tailed deer was killing a madly striking ground rattler with his sharp front hooves. Death was there, but it fitted, it belonged, it was part of a pattern. Panther was home, back in the world he knew and in which he could survive. His one sojourn out into the flat dry land where men had their enterprises had nearly ended in disaster. There was no place out there for him, not at this point in history. It had long ago been decided that only wastelands, at least lands considered waste, would be relatively safe for this continent's great predators. Inheritors of an incredibly ancient scheme of life, essential elements in any naturally constructed ecology, basic members of any wildlife community, they are the devils of human legend, the supposed anathema of human industry and the target against which mankind can seemingly best explode its own guilts, its own fear of natural inheritance.

Panther of the stealthy feet and the ghostlike pace, the huge yellow eyes and silken movements, was home, home in the Everglades, and here he would hunt, here he would kill, here he would plant his seed, and here he would one day die. The fact of his death would be far less significant than the fact of his birth, for he had come to be and caused others of his kind to do the same. And that was what nature had intended from the start. All the rest was of no account at all.